Who's In Charge?

A Positive Parenting Approach to Disciplining Children

Ruth A. Peters, Ph.D.

Lindsay Press • Clearwater, Florida

Inquiries about the content of this book should be addressed to Lindsay Press, Inc., P. O. Box 6316, Clearwater, FL 34618-6316

Library of Congress Catalog Card Number: 89-92329

ISBN: 0-9624728-0-8

To my family:

My parents for their foundation

My husband for his love and support

My children - just for being themselves

Acknowledgments

I wish to thank Myra Gunther for her typing and Harriet Coren for her preparation of the final copy after its many revisions. Appreciation is given to Technical Editor, Karen Schroeder for her support.

My special thanks to Roger Bansemer for the cover illustration.

Author's note

Names and identifying details in the case histories reported within the book have been changed. Any resemblance to persons living or dead is purely coincidental.

Foreword

The pages of this engaging book clearly reflect Dr. Ruth Peters' many years of experience as a clinical psychologist specializing in the diagnosis and remediation of child and adolescent emotional and behavioral problems. Written for both parents and child care professionals, Dr. Peters describes straightforward, practical and realistic approaches to child-rearing dilemmas that she has found to be effective in her successful clinical practice.

The major goals of *Who's In Charge? A Positive Parenting Approach to Disciplining Children* are to present understandable descriptions of child and adolescent behavioral problems through poignant anecdotes and descriptions and to provide coherent, workable solutions to these difficulties. These goals are attained in a remarkably clear and concise fashion. The reader is naturally led to the conclusion so aptly stated a decade ago by Dr. Scott Peck (*The Road Less Traveled*, 1978, pg. 19) "Discipline is the only way to live."

Families will be able to utilize the behavior management techniques described in this book to gain, or to regain, control of rebelling, noncompliant children. In addition to providing specific guidelines to success and solutions to possible obstacles, parents are given needed emotional support throughout the book.

While focusing upon the willfully noncompliant youngster, Dr. Peters also presents a thorough discussion of the epidemic problem of academic underachievement. Realistic study skill programs are presented in Chapter 4 that will enable parents, without further professional guidance, to help their youngsters achieve academic success by utilizing these programs.

Dr. Peters provides a comprehensive framework for understanding a vast range of childhood problems and discusses the Attention Deficit Disorders of hyperactive children in great detail. Medical, behavioral and educational management techniques are presented for coping with this debilitating disorder, which affects three to five percent of all school-aged children.

Children without self-discipline cannot achieve self-control and will inevitably grow up to be irresponsible adults. This book articulates the critical steps to be taken in developing healthy parent/child relationships that are essential to nurturing responsible adults for the 21st century.

Dr. Peters' text is one of the most comprehensive and useful works on child behavior management available today. Parents of children with behavioral problems as well as those with typical childhood dilemmas will find this book especially valuable.

Charles D. Spielberger, Ph.D.
President-Elect
American Psychological Association

Preface

"Help, my child is running the family!" is a concern voiced by many parents today. Mothers and fathers often feel powerless in dealing with their youngsters. Children can exhaust even the most well-intentioned parent and slowly the adult feels that it's not worth the battle.

When the parent loses the reins of control, the child loses the parent. Children without parents, or children whose parents have abdicated power, are youngsters without boundaries or guidelines.

When there are only few limits, the child sets the rules without the benefit of experience to guide the rule-making. Just as in political abdication, the child's takeover coup leads to chaos. Chaotic families abound, documenting the need for formalized parent training.

Parent training is necessary to assure that child take-over coups are kept to a minimum, and that if this has already occurred, the parents can learn how to regain control.

Although the battle field analogy noted above may seem extreme, many parents do feel weary as they progress through the stages of child-rearing. There are those, however, who seem to weather parenting successfully.

What are they doing differently? Dr. Fitzhugh Dodson, in his book entitled How to Discipline with Love (1978), suggests that these parents believe that how they parent will affect how their children behave, and accordingly they take care to consistently discipline their children.

Secondly, they are not afraid to confront their children, even if this means a temporary rift between the parent and child. Therefore, consistent discipline (the teaching of rules and consequences for maintaining or breaking rules) appears to be the key element. The parents' ability to accept negative emotions from the child, (for example, "I hate you for sending me to my room!") is essential.

Another group of successful parents appear to be those whose children possess good-natured temperaments. Everyone seems to know a family blessed with a youngster who appears by nature to be reasonable. Labor and childbirth were a breeze, the infant slept through the night after a few weeks and has been a sensitive, caring, achieving child ever since.

These families should count their lucky stars! Although these easygoing, self-motivated youngsters do exist, they appear to be the exception rather than the rule.

Psychological researchers continue to find evidence that temperament is largely inborn, that babies who are colicky and difficult tend to be stubborn and demanding youngsters (Kagan, 1987).

This does not mean that once the "blueprint" has been ascertained the parent should meekly accept it (for example, "My child was ornery from the beginning and therefore this is a lost cause"). In fact, quite the opposite is true.

Environmental influence can play an important part in molding personality and behavior. "Easy children" may need less molding (for example, a firm look from the parent may do the trick). Difficult children may need more guidance, such as Time-Outs, spankings or privileges removed. The trick is to be able to determine as early as possible which type of child one is raising and to utilize this information in developing the parent's disciplinary plan.

As well as being helpful for the naturally easygoing youngster, this book is especially geared for parents of difficult children; those who tend to be stubborn, noncompliant and demanding.

Although all of the techniques described herein are sound tactics for use with reasonable children, it may not be necessary to employ all of them with the naturally compliant youngster. However, even the most compliant child eventually reaches a "testy stage", a difficult phase in child development.

Some youngsters reach this stage later than others, but most will eventually evidence rebellious behavior. Parents need to be able to recognize the testy stage as a normal phase of development and to deal with it effectively. Guidelines for coping with "testing the limits" are presented throughout this book.

Putting others before one's self is the essence of self-discipline. It is the goal of this book to teach parents how to keep the reins of control without hindering their child's growth of independence and self-esteem.

If control has already been abdicated, parents--have heart! Parental control is just a few weeks away if one can inculcate and utilize the techniques presented herein.

Ruth A. Peters, Ph.D.

TABLE OF CONTENTS

CHAPTER 3
The Positive Parenting Approach to

CHAPTER 4
Academic Achievement:

CHAPTER 5

Chapter 1

Children Without Self-Discipline

*You are the bows from which your
children, as living arrows, are sent
forth.*

Kahlil Gibran

Psychologists have had the opportunity for over two
decades to view a very disturbing trend in child rearing
practices. In fact, the trend has begun to take epidemic
proportions. More and more children and adolescents
are lacking in self-control, are egocentric and display
poor frustration tolerance.

Many parents feel as if they are being held hostage by
their tykes. They resort to defensive postures due to
fear of conflict with their children, as well as guilt if
they do punish them. The incidence of dictatorial,
self-centered and demanding children appears to have
increased tremendously since the 1950's.

Why is this occurring? Perhaps it is based in parental
training. Many psychologists, pediatricians, and child
care workers have, in the past thirty years, been teaching parents that conflicts with their children are to be
viewed as differences of opinions and misunderstand-
ings.

In effect, parents have been taught to try to "reason with the unreasonable." This laissez-faire attitude trains parents to allow natural consequences to affect the child. Therefore parents are not being encouraged to give immediate consequences for the child's actions.

James Dobson, in his book <u>Dare to Discipline</u> (1982), notes that parents "Have read that a child will eventually respond to patience and tolerance, ruling out the need for discipline. . . Parents have been told to encourage the child's rebellion because it offered a valuable release of hostility."

According to Dobson, experts recommend that parents should verbalize or reflect the child's feelings in conflictual times, such as "You want the water, but you are angry because I brought it too late," as the child is dumping the water on the ground because she is frustrated.

Parental Strategies

Generally, parents respond to the parenting techniques they experienced themselves as children. They may mimic the parenting methods established by their own parents or try to parent in the opposite way since they feel that many mistakes were made long ago.

These individuals may go to great lengths to be giving and nonrestrictive with their children, since their parents (they feel) were too restrictive with them or they may feel that their parents were too lax with them and they are going to be rigid with their own children. Either way, these parents are not reacting to the individual needs of their current family but are listening to "old tapes" which may not pertain to the current situation.

Interspousal Resentment

When a new disciplinary system is discussed with parents, a relevant issue is the resentment that the parents have developed between themselves over the years. Generally, one parent blames the other for not being strict enough with the child. The mother may retort that the reason she is not strict is because she feels her husband is too firm with the youngster, and she is only trying to act as a "buffer" between father and daughter. The youngster initially becomes confused, but may notice the struggle between mother and father and may use it to her perceived advantage.

Another example is the youngster who is being punished by one parent and the other parent becomes involved in order to "save the child." Within a few minutes, it is obvious that the youngster has removed himself from the situation and the parents are now arguing. The argument may no longer be about the original issue, but may have been driven off-track. The parents proceed to rehash old situations, even those quite removed from what stimulated the current problem.

This has been seen time and time again in therapy and has often been pointed out to parents. They readily acknowledge that this process occurs but can't seem to remove themselves from the vicious cycle. The children also acknowledge what is occurring and youngsters have noted that they even depend upon this type of reaction from their parents in order to remove themselves from the situation, especially when the child is in "hot water."

Child Sabotaging Techniques

Another tactic which youngsters will use is that of guilt provocation. Youngsters know their parents' "hot buttons," as in the case of Linda and her father. Linda was in trouble for inappropriate behavior at school. After her father had finished lecturing her on why she should not talk back to her teachers, she erupted with, "I see you yelling at Mom, and nothing happens to you!"

Generally, this will catch the father off-guard, and the mother may subtly agree with the youngster (since this is something she most likely has been trying to discuss with the father for some time). The issue now turns to a spousal problem rather than a child/school problem.

Or, consider Andrew. Andrew knew that his mother was very anxious about his social relationships. He had noticed the pattern of his mother becoming sympathetic to his plight if it was one of social rejection or emotional instability. He stated to her that he had skipped class one day when the children began to tease him because of his new haircut.

However, the actual cause was that Andrew had not completed his homework assignment and did not wish to be given a detention. He had chosen the social rejection excuse because he knew that it would pull his mother off-track. His thinking was as follows, "If Mom does not see through the smoke screen, I may be able to convince her that this is why I skipped class."

If his mother had gone along with this, Andrew would have learned a very inappropriate lesson. The lesson being, "If I lie, I might be able to get away with it," as well as the experience that using guilt to manipulate and provoke people may temporarily accomplish one's needs.

Childhood As The Training Ground For Adult Behavior

Parents often do not realize that childhood is the training ground for adult development and behavior. The lessons they teach (both purposefully and inadvertently) to their children are quite long-lasting and often are permanent lessons which color their children's future adult behavior.

Even though parents will intellectually agree that what has been stated above makes sense, it can be very difficult for them to put it into practice, especially after years of letting their emotions control their behavior toward their children. It is extremely difficult for parents to take a risk and to behave in an alternative fashion with their youngsters. However, if the parent can change, so can the child, and both will benefit.

Jason

The case of Cathy, Robert and Jason is a typical situation illustrative of the plight in which parents often find themselves. Jason had been a beautiful, easy going baby, and Cathy and Robert felt that parenthood was not going to be as much of a chore as their friends and relatives had predicted.

Jason slept through the night before the end of his second month, nursed easily and took to solid foods very well. He always had a quick smile and even though he "seemed to be into everything," the loving way about the little boy melted their hearts.

It wasn't until the beginning of Jason's fourth year that Cathy and Robert became concerned with his behavior. They had given him everything they could in the material sense as well as their time, and especially in terms of attention. Jason, being their first and only child at that time, was showered with affection and the little boy was not in want for anything.

About the time of his fourth birthday, the parents noted that his behavior was becoming very demanding. In fact, he threw a temper tantrum at the birthday party in front of his playmates and relatives because he didn't receive a certain piece of cake. In order to quiet him down, Robert traded cake plates with one of Jason's friends so that Jason received the piece that he desired. That seemed to work but Jason was still grumpy following the incident.

Later that night, Robert and Cathy discussed Jason's behavior. Cathy tended to feel that he had misbehaved due to the excitement stimulated by his birthday presents, family and other invited guests, but Robert was not sure.

Robert had begun to see a trend in the evenings when he returned home from work. Cathy seemed to be continually frazzled and upset with Jason's behavior. She generally met Robert at the door looking very tired, as well as expressing exasperation. There were more and more evenings when Cathy would list the transgressions Jason had made. She appeared to be very frustrated, yet very guilty, regarding her relationship with her son.

Jason would whine and complain when he was told "No" and Cathy would resort to almost anything to try to quiet the child. The usual distractors (tickling, food treats) did not seem to be working as well as they had when he was a baby. Jason would stand his ground and had begun to bite and kick when his demands were not immediately met.

Cathy had tried reasoning with the youngster, explaining why she had to say "No" to him on occasion. She had even sent him to his room in one instance but Jason kept coming out. Cathy finally relented and gave him what he had originally wanted.

Robert was supportive of his wife since he did not know what to do either. This pattern of behavior increased to the time when Jason entered kindergarten.

In school, the teachers noted that Jason had difficulty remaining on tasks that he didn't like to do and would become disruptive to other children when he was bored.

Sitting on the circle line and listening to books were very difficult tasks for Jason, especially if the teacher was not reading a book that he particularly liked. He tended to have difficulty getting along with other youngsters since they did not cater to his needs and the parent/teacher conferences during kindergarten were becoming more negative. When he was in first grade, the school conferences became even more critical.

Cathy and Robert were willing parents in terms of doing anything that the school asked them to do, but everyone seemed to be throwing up their hands, wondering how to make Jason behave.

At home, Jason was becoming even more demanding in terms of tantrum behavior when he did not get his way. By the time Jason was seven-years-old and in second grade, Robert had begun to spank the child. This only seemed to anger Jason.

It was during this time that Cathy found out that she was pregnant again, and her happiness regarding the new baby was somewhat diminished due to the fear that another child would behave like Jason. She and Robert feared they would have to deal with two demanding, noncompliant youngsters. Cathy was also concerned that Jason would hurt the baby during a tantrum.

It was during Cathy's pregnancy that she and Robert had begun to talk to their pediatrician about getting help for the family. The pediatrician asked several questions about Jason's developmental milestones and his response to discipline. Cathy and Robert felt certain that no amount of discipline was going to help with their son. The pediatrician then recommended psychological counseling.

It took Cathy and Robert several weeks to decide to call as they were not sure that anyone could help with their disruptive son. The final straw came when Jason began to talk back to his second grade teacher and refused to come in from the playground at the end of recess. The school had asked the parents to consider placing Jason in a special educational program for noncompliant children since his behavior was becoming intolerable in the regular classroom.

That seemed to be the catalyst which Robert and Cathy needed in order to elicit the support and help from a psychologist.

The Positive Parenting Approach
To Disciplining Children

Jason and his parents present a scenario typical of families and youngsters who are commonly seen in counselors' offices. Parents feel that their youngster is controlling them and that the child is actually the one in charge. The problem is one of a lack of *consistent, effective parental discipline given in a nonchalant manner.*

The key words above are descriptors of the positive parental approach to disciplining children. If the parent does not provide this approach in the disciplinary process, then discipline will be less than successful.

Consistent, effective discipline given in a nonchalant manner is the goal. Just the thought of this sounds overwhelming! Parents with over-controlling, unself-disciplined children find it difficult to imagine that they could achieve this parental attitude.

Most families with noncompliant children have literally tried everything before seeking professional advice. Disciplinary tactics that they have employed often include spanking, Time-Out, removing privileges and most notably--lecturing.

Parents note that each of these consequences seem to work for a short time, but the effectiveness soon dissipates. The parents generally give in due to confusion and exhaustion. Parents come to the counselor's office at wits end, looking for a magic cure. They find that the cure is not magic. The solution involves common sense and effort, and is quite workable if the parents can employ consistent, effective discipline given nonchalantly. Let's discuss each of these descriptors separately.

Consistency

First, let's explore consistency. Most parents try to follow through with what rules they do establish, but many succumb to the sabotaging techniques of their children.

Youngsters are professionals at wearing parents down, and why shouldn't they be? They have more energy, the problem issue is usually very important to them and they generally have nothing more interesting to focus upon at the moment!

For example, eight-year-old Tommy continued to ask his mother if he could play outside even though it was close to dinner time.

Mother had said "No" three times and even threatened to send him to his room, but Tommy's persistence paid off as he continued to whine.

Mother finally threw up her hands and told him, "Just this once--but be back in fifteen minutes!" Another notch in Tommy's gun belt! There would be many more such incidents that would only serve to reinforce the inappropriate message, "If I wear her down by begging and bugging, I'll get my way."

Had mother stood her ground and placed Tommy in Time-Out (discussed in Chapter 2) he would have received another, more appropriate message. "When Mom says "No" she means it!"

Mother would have gained perhaps just an ounce of control, but ounces lead to pounds and we all know how difficult it is to lose a pound! In this case, the pounds are habits and expectations, that when established, lead to ways of perceiving rules and authority.

Alas, consistency is not always achievable. In some cases parents can only try to be as consistent as possible. Take the example of the divorced mother who is consistent when her children are with her, but who knows that during visitation with Dad, all rules go out of the window.

The parents should try to cooperate as much as possible and to devise a consistent set of parenting guidelines regardless of which parent is with the child. Parents must do their best to follow through so that children will not perceive parental statements as idle threats.

Effective Discipline

What are effective disciplinary tactics for one family may not be effective for another. Consequences are effective based upon such factors as the number of children in the family, the children's ages and the home environment.

In determining if a consequence is effective, the first question to ask is "Will the consequence make an impression on the child?" If it is a reward, is it appealing to the particular youngster? Tony may love building with blocks, but Mark may have four block sets and therefore may not feel that receiving more blocks is rewarding. Food treats may be appealing to Mary, whereas even candy may be snubbed by Joan and Barbara.

Punishments also must make an impression. The question regarding punishment should be, "Will this punishment be meaningful to the child?" Punishment does not mean harming the child in the physical sense, since corporal punishment usually is not effective in changing behavior for more than the immediate and it generally leads to poor parent/child relationships.

"Will it make an impression?" refers more to whether or not the negative consequence will bother the child. Fifteen minutes in Time-Out normally will not affect an eleven-year-old but one hour will, and if it doesn't, ninety minutes spent in Time-Out should make the youngster think twice!

13

Again, tailoring the consequence to the individual child is mandatory. A teenager who practically lives on the telephone will change almost any inappropriate behavior if telephone privileges are removed, whereas an introverted, shy youngster may respond more to the taking away of favorite books or hobbies.

Parental Nonchalance

Parents need to practice what is known as "parental nonchalance." This is a finely tuned response to children's inappropriate behaviors that displays little emotion on the parents' part. Failing to display nonchalance leads parents to being sure prey for their youngsters.

Children love to push their parents' hot buttons! What could be more controlling than merely talking back to an adult and seeing the parents' faces flush, arms move frantically and teeth clench? Some children delight in the control that they gain when they can cause so many physiological changes in an adult! It is almost worth the punishment and it certainly is quite entertaining to see an adult act in this manner.

Therefore, parents need to remove themselves from the cast of characters. They need to stay calm so that their emotional remote control box is not inadvertently handed over to the child.

In punishing youngsters, counselors suggest that parents quickly inform the youngster of the transgression, note the consequence and then enforce the punishment: quickly and without flinching!

Sound easy? No, it's not! It may take many weeks of practice but the payoffs are enormous. Children will no longer receive "points" for getting their parents angry; they will only receive negative consequences.

Couples seem to have an easier time achieving non-chalance than do single parents. When they feel that they are becoming unglued, one parent can hand the situation over to the other, take a break, and re-enter after gaining composure. This takes a lot of air out of the child's balloon when the youngster acts up mainly to disturb the adult. Again, it takes practice, but so do many of life's necessities.

Therefore, concurrent use of consistent, effective discipline given in a nonchalant fashion allows the parent to gain (or to regain) control and the family will become a more organized, pleasant unit.

How Parents Lose Control

It is interesting how parents get themselves into the situation of their children controlling the family. Most parents have very good intentions. They love their children greatly and will give them everything they can. They will give in the material sense, in terms of time, as well as in terms of giving attention to the child. The process seems to go awry when the parent gives in an *unconditional* manner. Parents tend to reward youngsters inadvertently for even very inappropriate behaviors.

For example, the teenager who continues to harass his parents to let him use the car even though his grades have been poor is typical. The parents may have already established that he will not be able to drive until he has achieved at least a "C" average in school.

Before he has accomplished this, he may have manipulated them into letting him use the car "just one more time." In this case, unconditional reward only serves to teach the child the inappropriate lesson that harassing and manipulating achieve one's goals.

Unconditional reward is generally based in caring, with parents wanting to give children whatever they can afford to give. In addition, unconditional reward is often used in an effort to avoid conflict. Most parents do not enjoy getting into arguments with their children and will tend to take the easy way out.

This may mean giving in to the child. Giving in teaches the youngster that inappropriate, demanding behavior can result in gaining their immediate goal. It is obvious, however, that this is not in the youngster's long-term best interest. The real world will not give in to temper tantrums and over-demanding behavior very often.

Therefore, the youngster may grow up without learning appropriate tactics to deal with frustration. Youngsters who do not learn how to take "No" for an answer tend to become adolescents who are impulsive and irresponsible.

They tend to develop without proper self-discipline and determination. These children, therefore, are plunged into adulthood without proper self-controls and are later seen as individuals with unstable work and marital histories. Learning to take "No" for an answer leads to the ability to deal with frustration, as well as acquiring task perseverance as an adult.

Frustration tolerance is not an innate personality characteristic. One must learn through the reactions of others (traditionally parents) to accept frustration and to look for appropriate solutions to one's problems.

Frustration Tolerance

Parents, although well-intentioned, tend to inadvertently allow children to delay development of frustration tolerance skills. For example, the four-year-old who demands to have a snack before supper and successfully harangues the parent into giving him one is not learning to tolerate frustration. He is learning a very inappropriate lesson that will lead to low frustration tolerance.

Although the parent, at the time, may feel that giving the child a snack before dinner will not have a significant effect upon the youngster, consistently giving in to inappropriate demands does have long-term consequences. The child's typical reaction to frustration will be to harangue, not to problem solve.

As parents, we tend to avoid dealing with conflict, and our children often make us feel guilty when things do not go their way. We ask ourselves "What would our parents have done in this situation?" or "What will be the effect on my child if I do not allow him to have what he is asking for or to do what he wants to do?"

17

In an effort to do the best job that we can, parents often give their children too much. "Too much" includes too many material objects, too many freedoms and too much control. In the process of giving our children too much, parents are not giving them enough of a very important value--the value of self-control.

Self-control is accomplished by parents creating boundaries and limits for their children. The old adage, "It was almost as if he was asking to be punished," is quite apt. One often sees children who appear to be happier after they have been punished and limits have been set for them. Children usually do not seek limit setting, but their temperaments improve when they know what they can get away with and what they can't.

For example, Marcia consistently begged her parents to allow her to stay up later at night. Her parents felt that 8:30 p.m. was an appropriate bedtime for a seven-year-old, but Marcia often didn't get to bed until 9:30 p.m.

After attending counseling and learning about limit setting, her parents were able to set strict guidelines. Marcia was in bed by 8:30 p.m. and following two weeks of a firm commitment to this bedtime by her parents, she actually slept better, awoke with a better attitude and was a more reasonable child since she was receiving more rest.

Once the boundary had been set, Marcia was able to abide by it. Her parents had consistently demanded compliance with the rule and Marcia was a happier child.

Parenting as a Benevolent Dictatorship
Rather Than as a Democracy

Mothers and fathers find that parenting as a "benevolent dictatorship" rather than parenting as a "democracy" to be the most effective manner of teaching children frustration tolerance and self-control. The parent has greater control and establishes more stability in the home.

The child learns frustration tolerance, which is a skill of immeasurable value in terms of the effects that it will have throughout the youngster's life. When the child learns that the parent will set the limits and establish the boundaries rather than the child having the final vote, it is easier for the youngster to be able to accept rules that do not please him later in life. This is extremely important to the adult in work and marital situations.

In becoming a "benevolent dictator" the parent learns that although he may feel guilty and perhaps sorry for the child when he has to punish the youngster, the child will profit from receiving the consequence rather than being taught the wrong lesson. (The wrong lesson being that behavior does not lead to predictable consequences.)

Youngsters who grow to adulthood not having learned the skills of self-control and frustration tolerance tend to become unsuccessful, unstable adults. We must, therefore, teach the parent in order to teach the child.

Chapter 2

General Guidelines for Behavior Management

Where parents do too much for children, the children will not do much for themselves.
                                    Elbert Hubbard

"Well-behaved children are much easier to love and appreciate than those who constantly flout your rules--a child's misbehavior is simply an exercise of power-- doing what he or she wants to do in the absence of active parental authority." (Bodenhamer, 1988, Preface.)

If-Then Children

Misbehavior or noncompliance are the most character- istic behaviors of what may be described as *if-then* children.

Most children are *if-then* kids. If you are one of the lucky parents whose first born is not an *if-then* kid, you are the exception and should be quite thankful! But watch out, your next one will most likely bear the *if-then* trademark!

What is an *if-then* kid? This is the child who will respond only if the parent says something to the effect of, "*If* you don't stop this behavior, *then* I will punish you." Most children need to know the consequences of their actions before they make their decision as to whether they will act-out or act appropriately.

Parents continually claim that this was not the way it was when they were growing up as a child. There are various versions of the tale, but most proceed as follows, "When I was a kid, I wouldn't dare talk back to my parents or my father would have walloped me."

Another rendition is, "I did what my mother asked me to do just because she was my mother and I was expected to comply." No doubt there are many adults today who truly acted appropriately as children. No doubt, however, there were many *if-then* children in their generation also.

Most of us were acquainted with *if-then* children as we were growing up. These were the youngsters who continually broke rules and tried to push the limits as much as possible. If their parents or teachers were not successful at consistently applying consequences for unacceptable behaviors, these *if-then* children of long ago have most likely evolved into *if-then* adults today.

If-then adults still continue to need rules to keep their behavior appropriate. "*If* you have an affair, *then* I will leave you," is typical of the wife of an *if-then* husband. This threat may or may not be successful, depending upon whether the *if-then* husband values the marital relationship.

Another version would be, "*If* you do not come to work on time, *then* I will fire you." Too many *if-then* employees lose their jobs because the threat of being without a job is not important enough to them or they are lacking in the self-control necessary to follow the rules given by the employer.

Today's parents need to disregard their perception of the way they acted toward their parents when they were children and to focus more upon the ways in which their own children are behaving.

To expect the child to be reasonable because "that's the way it should be" or "that's the way I was for my parents" is unrealistic and illusionary.

Practical parenting involves the perception of one's children in a realistic manner and therefore one must develop realistic expectations for them.

If a parent is lucky enough to have a reasonable child, reasoning with the youngster will most likely be effective. Even the most reasonable of children will become an *if-then* child occasionally. However, if the frequency of acting-out is low, occasional outbursts are generally tolerable.

It is the child who continually needs the *if-then* parental approach who wears down the parent but the adult must persevere by continually responding with very clear rules. This is necessary if the parent is to continue to control the situation.

When the parent becomes exhausted and gives in, the child's tendencies to try to manipulate the parent are bolstered. In other words, the parent must learn to outmanipulate the manipulator.

Rule Setting

In Chapter 3, detailed Behavior Management Techniques are presented for children of various ages. These techniques will serve the parent well when used in a consistent manner. Before proceeding to the specific behavior management systems, a presentation of general rule-setting techniques is in order.

Grandma's Rule

A very important principle in rule-setting is known as the Premack Principle, commonly referred to as Grandma's Rule, most likely because our foremothers tended to employ it liberally.

Grandma's Rule states, "After you do your work, then you will get to play." A variant of this is, "After you do your homework, then you can watch television or go outside." However, parents tend to reverse Grandma's Rule in terms of negotiating with their children.

For instance, the child may promise upon a stack of video cartridges that he will do his homework if only he can play his video game first. As many parents find out, the odds of the child completing his homework after he has played the video game are slim.

Then the parent must reason with an unmotivated child (since he has already received his reward) and she finds herself having been manipulated by the youngster. In this case, the *if-then* child has sabotaged Grandma's Rule and has inadvertently been rewarded for his lack of performance and procrastination.

Rules for good parenting include:

- Consistently rewarding good behavior and doing so immediately

- Being sure to punish inappropriate behavior, and using an effective punisher such as Time-Out

- Not rewarding inappropriate behavior

Let's delve further into each of these rules. Rewarding good behavior and doing so immediately is very important. For example, the parent who has been struggling with his youngster to complete dinner at the table without constantly leaving his chair is a typical problem situation. One evening, the youngster remains at the table for six minutes and instead of merely ignoring this behavior, the parent chooses to note it.

Father states, "You sat there for over five minutes, that is terrific! Because you've done so well you will receive dessert tonight." In this example, the child who had previously continued to leave the table in a consistent manner chose to remain seated. Father grabbed this opportunity to reward him verbally. In addition, the parent rewarded immediately following the child's appropriate behavior.

However, had the child continued to leave the table, the father should have given him a negative consequence since the child had previously been warned that leaving the table without permission was inappropriate.

The latter would be an example of the second rule, that of punishing undesirable behavior. It should be noted that the above example offers either a reward (verbal praise) or a punishment and these are given immediately, concisely and clearly.

It cannot be overstated that both reward and punishment must be fair, consistent and most important-- immediate.

Immediacy of consequences is particularly important for toddlers and younger children who may misinterpret why they are being rewarded or punished if the length of time between behavior and consequence is too long.

The third rule involves inadvertently rewarding inappropriate behavior. The parent who gives in to his youngster's constant whining and complaining is a typical example of inadvertent rewarding of undesirable behavior.

Children have a tremendous ability to persevere. They can hassle a parent endlessly, especially if, in the past, the parent has given in to the child's demands. Whining and crying are not nearly as adversive to the child as not getting what he wants.

However, the opposite appears to be true for most parents. Having to listen to whining and crying is often more intolerable than just giving in to the youngster. The solution to this problem is placing the child in Time-Out after giving appropriate warnings.

Time-Out

Time-Out is both a physical and a psychological situation. Physically, a Time-Out setting is a safe and boring place where the child must go for a specified time. Psychologically speaking, Time-Out is the placement of the child away from all attention and all interesting activities.

This allows the youngster to consider what rule he has broken in order to have been placed in Time-Out, as well as to think about how to avoid being placed in Time-Out in the future.

Setting

The optimal Time-Out situation is a guest bedroom but any room will suffice if it is emptied of interesting or potentially dangerous objects. One must look for scissors, sewing materials, etc., and remove these from the room since the child, when placed in Time-Out, may be quite angry and inadvertently harm himself.

The youngster is then placed in the Time-Out room for a set period of time. The amount of time varies according to the age of the child. The toddler may be in Time-Out for only a few minutes, whereas the seven-year-old usually needs ten to fifteen minutes of Time-Out for his misdeed to sink in. The adolescent may need thirty to sixty minutes in Time-Out to gain his attention.

Keeping the Child in Time-Out

Some youngsters need to have the door closed during Time-Out since they tend to leave the room. If the child opens the door and leaves the room, then the door may need to be locked. This will eliminate parents having to continually become involved in replacing him in the Time-Out situation.

It is suggested that the child be given little or no attention during Time-Out. Youngsters need to learn that their parents are in control and will resort to placing them in a boring, safe situation when the child loses self-control or becomes overly demanding. If a guest room is not available, a bathroom or the child's bedroom may suffice.

Again, it is mandatory that all potentially harmful objects be removed so the child does not hurt himself. For instance, if bathroom Time-Out is employed, all of the cleaning materials, towels, etc., need to be removed because these can be either fun or potentially dangerous. The water may need to be turned off so that the child will not scald himself.

Many parents remove faucet handles and leave only the toilet working, so that the child has access to it if necessary and therefore has no excuse to request leaving the bathroom.

It is important to remember that the purpose of Time-Out is to gain the child's attention, not to place him in a harmful environment. Whenever the Time-Out situation is employed, it must be safe, boring, well-lit and well-ventilated. Time-Out is effective by boring the child, not by harming the youngster.

Use of the Timer

Therefore, some Time-Out situations will involve a locked Time-Out room for fifteen minutes or more, depending upon the age of the child. The use of a timer is also suggested for Time-Out. The timer is placed outside of the room and is set for the allotted period. The child will know when Time-Out is over when the buzzer rings and the parent removes the child from the situation only at that time.

This eliminates the need for the parent to respond to the child's persistent questions, "Is it time yet?" or "When can I come out?" The less the parent communicates with the youngster during Time-Out, the better.

This is an example of the parental nonchalant attitude and is very important during Time-Out. If the child perceives that he has the parent upset, the youngster may feel that he has won the conflict.

In reality, no one wins in control conflicts. These situations should be looked upon as learning experiences, not as notches on a gun barrel by either the parent or the youngster.

The parent will experience that Time-Out is a powerful technique used to quickly regain the parent's composure and to emphasize to the child that the parent is in control.

Time-Out Must Be Safe

It is imperative though, that during Time-Out the parent listen to the child so that if the youngster does hurt himself, aid can be given immediately.

The emptier the room, the more safe it is. Parents are even encouraged to remove the child's sneakers upon entering Time-Out so that the youngster does not throw them against windows or walls, potentially knocking down objects.

The goal of Time-Out is to have the child in a boring situation, not a dangerous one.

It is interesting to note that some youngsters, when they are allowed to leave the Time-Out situation after the timer has rung, tend to appear to be more angry than they were when they went in. Often they will fuss, kick and hit due to the anger of being placed in Time-Out.

This is another good time for parental nonchalance. The parent can quietly let the child know that he has misbehaved again. Therefore, he may be placed back in Time-Out if the inappropriate behavior continues.

Some children periodically need extended Time-Out, perhaps for twenty or twenty-five minutes before they realize that they are even in an uncomfortable situation and they will not want to place themselves in it again.

The child needs to realize that it is he who is placing himself in Time-Out, not the parent!

Time-Out accomplishes two purposes: It relieves the parents of having to listen to the child's incessant fussing. It also teaches the youngster that there is an immediate consequence for his inappropriate behavior.

This is also referred to as response cost. In this case, the youngster has learned that fussing and crying are just not worth it. The fussing behavior did not achieve what he wanted and he also had to pay for it by being placed in Time-Out.

Types of Rewards

In terms of rewarding youngsters, there are several options that parents have which are effective. Activity, social and material rewards are the most common reinforcers.

Activity Rewards

Activity or privilege rewards can be quite effective with youngsters. Toddlers enjoy going to the park, having a story read to them or being tickled. Young children enjoy playing catch with a ball, going for a bike ride and having a parent play a board game with them.

Teenagers enjoy the privilege of playing video games, being allowed time with their friends or having their parents provide transportation to a mall or to a friend's house. The telephone is also an extremely effective activity reward.

Social Rewards

Social rewards are types of attention such as hugs and praise. Children crave parental approval and will work to receive it. Younger children enjoy touching (hugs and kisses) whereas teenagers prefer being praised for a job well done.

Material Rewards

The third major type of reward includes material objects. Toddlers enjoy stickers and food treats. Young children enjoy snacks, building sets (the parent can give a few pieces of the set as a reward each day for good behavior) and poker chips which, when added up, can result in a trip to the toy store at the end of the week.

Teenagers greatly enjoy material rewards such as clothing and money. "Clothing poker chips" can be extremely effective.

The parent determines approximately how much money is spent for the child's clothing during a one month, six month, or one year duration. It is then decided how much this would equal on a daily basis.

For example, if the parent determines that she spends approximately $600.00 per year on clothing for the youngster, then the poker chip earned daily may be worth approximately $2.00. The child can then earn one clothing poker chip per day as part of a Behavior Management System. This amount is to be spent for clothing only.

One of the outcomes of this technique is that children learn to spend money wisely. Initially, many children tend to be extravagant and buy expensive designer clothing.

However, when they realize that the parent is not going to be buying any other clothing for them (except for essentials) then the child usually begins to look for sales and will become more prudent in the spending of her money.

The parent is cautioned to not overparent by interfering with the child's selections. She has to learn how to handle the spending of money herself, even if mistakes are made at the beginning of the clothing poker chip system.

Chapter 3

The Positive Parenting Approach to Behavior Management Systems

*Children have never been very good
at listening to their elders, but they
have never failed to imitate them.*
James Baldwin

For decades, psychologists have proposed many forms
of motivational strategies in an effort to teach self-
control. It has been found that reasoning with youngsters is generally not the most efficient manner of
instilling self control.

Youngsters, quite often, are egocentric and unreasonable and therefore *reasoning with the unreasonable* may not work. The parent must decide what
behaviors one wants from the child and then devise a
plan that will most likely achieve the desired results.

Many approaches to child rearing have been suggested
by child care workers. These approaches range from
reflecting the child's feelings to Behavior Modification
Systems.

Research on the outcome of the various techniques
consistently suggests that Behavior Modification Systems
are the most efficient and permanent methods of
changing inappropriate behavior (Silverman and Lustig
(1987); Dobson (1982).

Developed in the laboratory, Behavior Modification determined that researchers could greatly modify the behavior of rats, monkeys and even fish. If fish can be taught to behave according to the desires of the researcher, then certainly children's behavior should be able to be modified by parents!

Chapter 2 presented general rules for Behavior Modification and parents should become familiar with them as a guideline to dealing with their children on an everyday basis.

However, just following "general guidelines" does not provide a program specific enough for many noncompliant youngsters.

Literally dozens of parenting guides have been written proposing adherence to general rules that will change children's behaviors. However, general principles do not offer enough detail to aid parents in setting up an effective Behavior Management System.

Therefore, a very specific Behavior Management System is presented next; one that has been found to be highly successful with children seven years through adolescence.

Following that is a section which presents a Behavior Management System for children three through six years of age (The Smiley Face System).

The Behavior Management System for Children Seven Years of Age Through Adolescence

This system involves five basic sections:

- Daily Expectations

- Behavior/Attitude Bad Points

- Criteria for a "Good Day"

- Consequences for Behavior

- Guidelines for Time-Out

Each of these will be explained in detail and followed by an example of the Behavior Management System set up for Jason and his parents, the family previously discussed in Chapter 1.

Daily Expectations

Each family has various chores and expectations that they would like their children to perform. Generally, parents set up these expectations in some form for their children, either verbally or in a written context.

On the Behavior Management System the Daily Expectations are listed vertically on a chart so that they can be checked each day as to whether they have been accomplished appropriately (see Page 38).

Home Behavior Management System

Daily Rewards		Weekly Rewards	Codes
$.25	Parent Time (15 min.)	Need at least five	* = On Time
Electricity	Grab Bag Prize	Good Days:	* = Correctly
Freedom	Bedtime 8:00/9:00	(1) Stay up later	* = No Hassle
Bedtime Snack	Poker Chip	(2) One Special Activity	✔ = Bad Point

Daily Expectations	Sat	Sun	Mon	Tue	Wed	Thu	Fri	Sat	Sun	Mon	Tue
Go to bed well	*	*	*	*							
Get dressed (5 min.)	*	*	*	*							
Make bed (5 min.)	*	*	*	*							
Put P.J.'s away	X	*	*	*							
Brush teeth and hair	*	*	*	X							
Eat breakfast well	*	*	X	*							
Bring school things in	*	*	X	*							
"Daily Report Card"	*	*	X	*							
Homework done well	*	*	*	*							
Daily chore	X	*	*	*							
House pick-up (5 min.)	*	*	X	X							
Clean bedroom (5 min.)	*	X	X	*							
Bathe & clean bathroom	*	X	*	*							
Bad Points (allow 6 or 8)											
Not doing as told	✔✔	✔✔	✔	✔							
Not taking "No" well		✔✔	✔	✔							
Talking back	✔		✔	✔							
Interrupting	✔			✔							
Fighting		✔✔		✔							
Tattling		✔		✔							
Fussing		✔									
Coming home late		✔									
Good Day? Needs at least 11 *'s and 6/8 or less Bad Points	*	X	X	*							

3 Bad Points in a row = 10 minutes Time-Out

9/11 or more Bad Points = Child goes to bedroom immediately for remainder of the day

The youngster is given credit with a star (* noted on chart) for appropriate accomplishment if the expectation or chore has been completed correctly, on time and cooperatively.

If this is done, the child receives a star for completion of that chore. If it is not completed correctly, on time and cooperatively, the child then receives an "X" and is still made to perform the chore.

This teaches the child that he will perform the expectancy but will not receive credit unless he does it cooperatively. This will generally motivate the youngster to be responsible in terms of chore achievement.

Chores with which parents are concerned can range from the very specific to the very general. When using the Behavior Management System, it is suggested that the chart be quite specific so that there is no ambiguity regarding what is to be accomplished.

Therefore, the following list is quite detailed, perhaps more so than necessary for many families. These expectations are typical.

Chores may be added or deleted as the family individualizes the Daily Expectations for their own needs.

Examples of Daily Expectations

- Go to bed the night before in a cooperative manner

- Get up on time

- Get dressed (ten minutes)

- Make bed/put pajamas away (five minutes)

- Brush teeth, wash face, brush hair

- Clean up after breakfast

- Leave for school appropriately

- Put school articles away following school

- Complete homework cooperatively

- Come in by 6:00 p.m. from outside play

- Dinner chore

- House pick-up (ten minutes)

- Bedroom clean-up (ten minutes)

- Put clothes out for the next day

- Take a bath and clean bathroom

- Brush teeth

Time Limits

As may be noted from the above list some of the chores have time limits. A portable timer, which is an inexpensive device that can be bought at most grocery stores, is an invaluable asset for use in the Behavior Management System.

The child's idea of completing a chore in a timely manner is often quite different from the parent's idea. Therefore, the parent starts the timer when the chore time is to begin. It is not the child who determines when "house pick-up" should start.

For example, the child is told by the parent, "I am going to set the timer for bedroom clean-up now. You have exactly ten minutes to clean up your room. Go!"

The child then has those ten minutes to completely clean up the bedroom.

It has previously been discussed with the child that a clean bedroom means there are no articles left on the floor, what was on the floor is not to be stuffed in the closet nor under the bed, all drawers are to be closed and the desk top is fairly neat. The parent does not expect the child to dust nor vacuum each day, but the bedroom is to be neat and orderly.

If, upon inspection after the timer rings, the parent notes a sneaker in one corner of the room, the child must then place the shoe in the appropriate spot in the closet, but receives an "X" on his chart since the task was not performed completely. Or, if the child finishes the task in eleven minutes rather than ten minutes, the youngster is also not given credit since the time limit must be established and maintained.

The Daily Expectation portion of the chart must be quite rigid, since many children, if given areas of ambiguity, will abuse them. Ten minutes means ten minutes, it does not mean eleven or twelve minutes.

The "Be home by 6:00 p.m." Daily Expectation is an example of this. Six o'clock means 6:00 p.m. on the kitchen clock, not on the child's watch (which can always be set five minutes late with the child then arguing that he was on time according to his own watch).

Rigidity is extremely important when employing Daily Expectations since many children will try to manipulate the system if at all possible. When beginning the Behavior Management System, all of the Daily Expectations must be defined and explained thoroughly to the child so that there is no question as to what the youngster must do to receive a star.

If the expectation is not applicable that day, such as "there is no homework due on Saturday," the child then receives a star for that item even though he did not have to complete anything. Therefore, there is never a blank space for a Daily Expectation.

The youngster either performed it on time, correctly and cooperatively and received a star, or the child received an "X" for that item by not having performed it appropriately.

If the expectation was not applicable for that day, the child receives a star (again, see Page 38).

Behavior/Attitude Bad Points

The Behavior/Attitude section involves Bad Points (✓) being given to youngsters for inappropriate behaviors or attitudes that the parent wishes to decrease. The child is allowed a designated maximum number of Bad Points per day.

When beginning a system, it is typical to allow six Bad Points on a school day and eight Bad Points on a weekend or holiday (since the child is with the parent for a greater amount of time during the weekend). The child must keep the number of Bad Points to the allotted amount or less to maintain a "Good Day" (to be discussed below).

The parent is encouraged to be very strict in giving out Bad Points, since if the child feels that the parent will look the other way, the system will be ineffectual.

For example, if the problem behavior is that of "Talking Back," and one parent feels that the child spoke inappropriately but the other parent did not perceive it as such, it is suggested that the child be given a "Talking Back" Bad Point.

In this fashion the youngster will understand that his parents will not tolerate "Talking Back" nor inappropriate verbal behavior.

43

Examples of Behavior/Attitude Bad Points

- Not doing as told the first time

- Not taking "No" for an answer

- Talking Back

- Rudeness

- Interrupting

- Fighting/Teasing

- Tattling

- Taking things without permission

- Lying

- Stealing

- Leaving without permission

- Bugging/Hassling

While the above addresses typical Behavior/Attitude Bad Points, individual families may decide to delete some and to add others. As can be seen from this list of misdeeds, it is only the tip of the iceberg in terms of possible inappropriate behaviors!

However, this list addresses the most frequent parental complaints as well as causes for reprimands according to children.

An example of, "Not doing as told the first time," is as follows: Father tells Johnny to put his magazines in his bedroom. Johnny responds, "In a minute, Dad" but does not move. Dad notes, "That's <u>One</u>" as he puts a small check mark next to the "Not doing as told the first time" column on the chart. Father then says to Johnny, "You've got <u>One</u>, now put your magazines in your bedroom."

Johnny does not bother to respond this time. Father places a second check mark in the same column on the chart, and says, "Johnny that's <u>Two</u>, now put your magazines in the bedroom." Johnny now retorts, "I said in a minute, Dad!" and still makes no movement toward the magazines.

Father notes, "John, that's <u>Three</u>" and puts the third mark on the chart.

If a child will not comply by the third request, then the youngster will most likely not comply upon the tenth request!

Therefore, if the child receives three Bad Points in a row, the youngster will be placed in Time-Out for ten minutes in an effort to break the stubbornness of the moment. (Time-Out situations were discussed beginning on Page 27.) Upon leaving the Time-Out situation, the magazine issue is dropped but Johnny has received three Bad Points out of his allowed six for that day.

45

This example is used to describe how a youngster can achieve more than one Bad Point for the same inappropriate behavior in quick succession. The parent need not be afraid to give Bad Points when the child deserves them!

It should be noted that severe offenses such as lying and stealing can be allotted an automatic three or four Bad Points for each incident. Exaggerations may be seen as one Bad Point, but telling the parent that the child had to stay after school for a soccer match when in reality he stayed for a detention is a lie; that may be worth three or four Bad Points in and of itself.

This is an individual decision that each family needs to make as they are developing the Bad Point section of the Behavior Management System, as seen on Page 38.

Fighting and Teasing

Another area of considerable concern is fighting and teasing. Most families have come to recognize that siblings fight and that they fight constantly. If they are not fighting, then they are teasing.

When the parent asks the child, "Who started the fight?" the response is usually that the other person started it and then an argument generally ensues. To avoid this senseless situation, the fighting and teasing rule is: "Anybody involved in a fight or a tease receives a Bad Point."

To further establish that the parent does not wish to hear about teasing and fighting, the children are told that the person who tattles about the fight receives an additional Bad Point under the column marked, "Tattling."

The youngsters are informed that it is appropriate to notify parents if a sibling is performing an illegal or dangerous action. That is not tattling. It is looking out for the welfare of the sibling.

However, most tattling incidents involve the continuation of the fighting or teasing and generally serve no purpose. Therefore, an additional tattling Bad Point following the fighting Bad Point usually calms the situation down.

This rigid fighting/teasing/tattling rule generally results in children either fighting quietly, fighting when parents are not around, or more appropriately, beginning to fight less since it is not worth it!

Most sibling battles occur out of boredom or because children enjoy fighting. If they begin to receive Bad Points for this behavior, fighting generally becomes less intriguing.

Criteria for a "Good Day"

To achieve a "Good Day" on the Behavior Management System, the youngster must have performed appropriately in both the Daily Expectation section and the Behavior/Attitude Bad Point section.

A "Good Day" involves achieving a minimal number of stars on the Daily Expectation section, such as 11 out of a possible 13 chores completed appropriately. This indicates that the youngster has produced a good effort to complete the chores.

In addition, the child must have kept the number of Bad Points to the maximal allowable level or less (for example, six Bad Points on a school day or eight Bad Points on a weekend.) Then the child would have earned a "Good Day" star at the bottom of the chart. The "Good Day" star line is written underneath the Behavior/Attitude Bad Points section. This line is never blank.

The child either received a "Good Day" for having at least 11 of his stars on the chart and six or eight Bad Points or less (depending upon the day of the week) or the youngster did not meet the criteria for both sections of the chart (Daily Expectations and Behavior/Attitude Bad Points) and the child received an "X" on the "Good Day" line.

Timing of the "Good Day" Star

The establishment of whether a day is a "Good Day" or not can occur at any point. If the child, for instance, received his ninth Bad Point at 2:00 on Saturday afternoon, then at that moment the child knows his chart will be marked with an "X" for the "Good Day" category.

At that point he realizes there will be no Daily Rewards for the remainder of the day. If he has received some rewards prior to 2:00 p.m., then there is nothing that the parent can do about this. The parent must then focus upon making certain the child receives no further rewards that day.

The child begins a new day the next morning and the only thing carried over from one day to the next is the first line on the Daily Expectation section noting "Go to bed well" from the night before.

If the child achieves a "Good Day" star on the chart near bedtime, he receives all of the Daily Rewards. If the child does not earn a "Good Day" star on the chart, then the youngster does not receive any of the Daily Rewards that would be given for the rest of the day.

Consequences: Rewards and Punishments

The rewards and punishments are divided into Daily Rewards and Weekly Rewards. The Daily Rewards are listed on the top left side of the chart, and the Weekly Rewards are listed in the center of the chart.

Daily Rewards

In setting up the Daily Rewards, the child is generally the main source of information. Children often have quite different attitudes as to what each feels is rewarding. Generally, younger children desire food treats, grab bag prizes (trinkets), stickers and television privileges.

Older children tend to enjoy food treats, television and video privileges, staying up later at night and access to the telephone. It should be noted that a core principle of behavior management is to offer what is appealing to the youngster, not necessarily what the parents feel to be rewarding.

Some Daily Rewards are enticing to children but can be somewhat difficult for parents to provide. One such reward is that of "parent time." This involves the child earning fifteen minutes of one parent's time later in the evening when the parent must play any game that the child wishes to play.

Children enjoy this tremendously but it is often difficult for the parent to provide. However, if the parent offers this as a reward for the child, the parent must be consistent and provide it to the youngster.

Another powerful incentive is that of poker chips. In a family with more than one child, each youngster can be assigned a certain color chip. For example, Mary can receive blue chips, John may receive red chips and Matthew may receive white chips. In this fashion, if chips are "borrowed" it can easily be established to which child the chip should be returned.

Poker chips can be used for privilege rewards (cashing in ten chips to go to the park, seven to be taken to a friend's house outside of the neighborhood) or can be used for staying up later (four chips to stay up one-half hour later to watch television).

In addition, poker chips can be used for clothing purchases. Teenagers especially enjoy the routine of accumulating clothing poker chips so they can buy articles of clothing that parents may feel to be unnecessary, but that youngsters deem vital.

This may include T-shirts advertising musical groups or other articles of clothing that are not necessities but which are very important to the youngster.

The parent and the child establish the monetary value of a poker chip that can be traded in for money at the time the child goes to the store to purchase the article.

Another effective reward for children seven years and older is that of a daily allowance. Most parents, if they were to calculate what they spend on their child weekly, would be amazed at how much they spend for candy, gum and soft drinks.

Children can be incredibly persistent and can hassle parents into buying them trinkets and food treats when they are in stores and malls.

Therefore, if the child is given a daily allowance (the amount depending upon the age of the youngster) he can use this money if he wishes to purchase these items.

For example, a fourteen-year-old may receive $1.00 a day allowance whereas an eight-year-old may receive $.50 a day. When the eight-year-old is at the grocery store with the mother and insists upon buying a rubber ball for $1.49, the mother can suggest that the child use his own money if he really wants it.

Sometimes the child will decide to use his own money, but parents will be surprised at how often the youngster will begin to think about the necessity of such purchases when the money comes out of his own pocket!

Therefore, using an allowance as a reward can be a very good learning experience for the youngster in terms of appreciating the value of money as well as stopping parent/child store arguments.

Weekly Rewards

Weekly Rewards are earned if the child receives at least five "Good Days" out of seven during a week. A week technically begins on Saturday morning and ends Friday night. The child can begin to consider what Weekly Reward he wishes to achieve the next weekend, possibly beginning to think about it on the previous Wednesday or Thursday.

Weekly Rewards involve staying up later on Friday and Saturday nights, having a friend spend the night, going skating, going to the movies or picking the restaurant to go out to dinner.

If a Good Week has not been accomplished (less than five "Good Days" during that week) the child does not stay up later on Friday and Saturday nights, is not grounded, but may not play out of the neighborhood during the weekend. The parents should make sure that the weekend is boring.

This brings up a typical comment made by youngsters when they first learn of the Behavior Management System. Many complain they will now have to work for items and activities they were heretofore allowed to engage in without having to earn.

Many children are allowed to stay up later on the weekends, have friends spend the night, go to the mall and receive allowances without having to accomplish any tasks. When the Behavior Management System is employed they now have to complete chores plus behave appropriately. Some react negatively since they feel they are "not getting anything out of the deal," whereas others are more cooperative.

The most effective parental response is to note that the parents are going to adhere to the rules of the Behavior Management System and if the child does not want to, it is the child's choice, but he will not receive his Daily or Weekly Rewards.

Some very stubborn youngsters will commit to not going along with the program for a week or two, but after they see that they are not receiving their allowance, that they have no television nor telephone privileges, that they are not allowed to play outside of the home, they will begin to cooperate.

Parental consistency and nonchalance are very important in handling the Behavior Management System. If the parent can outlast the child, the child will eventually give in and will display much more appropriate behavior.

When Only One of the Children Earns a Weekly Reward

Another concern of parents is what to do if one youngster earns a Weekly Reward and the other youngster doesn't. This is an excellent learning situation for both children. The child who has earned the Weekly Reward should receive it and the child who hasn't should not.

For example, the child with the Good Week may choose to go roller skating and the youngster with the Bad Week may either remain at home or could go to the skating rink but not be allowed to skate. Either way, both children will see that their behavior effects what happens to them.

There are many barriers to parental consistency and children will try to manipulate parents into disregarding the charting system. However, if the parents are consistent they should see excellent results within two weeks and the program will become self-rewarding.

Many parents remark that they feel embarrassed for not embarking on such a program before. Other parents note that they have tried similar systems but the pro-grams were not as concrete nor as detailed. Therefore the children were able to outmanipulate the parents.

The Child is Responsible For His Behavior

It is imperative that parents realize the Behavior Management System involves the child's relationship with his own behavior via the chart and not with the parent's behavior or emotions. If this is accomplished, the child will begin to take more responsibility for his own actions. Parents need to consistently note to the child, "Because you have done well on the chart today," or "Because you have earned a Good Day on the chart, here are your rewards."

Jason's Behavior Management System

In working with Cathy, Robert and seven-year-old Jason in developing the Behavior Management System, the family had typical responses to the various sections of the program. Jason questioned why he would have to work for rewards that he had previously received automatically and he felt the system was unfair.

Cathy and Robert were interested in establishing the chores and expectations for Jason, but they were somewhat doubtful as to whether Jason would cooperate. They were told to have a positive attitude and to expect Jason to achieve his Daily Expectations. His behavior would be a barometer of their own consistency in following the chart!

Cathy and Robert focused upon the inappropriate behaviors of talking back, not doing as told the first time and not taking "No" for an answer. Jason had an incredible ability to argue when he was not given his way and Cathy and Robert were interested in gaining control over these specific behaviors. They also suggested giving Bad Points for interrupting, complaining and fussing.

Robert questioned what would happen if Jason lost his "Good Day" for example, at 3:00 p.m. on Saturday and realized he had lost all of his Daily Rewards. Robert speculated that Jason would probably misbehave for the remainder of the day.

It was suggested to the parents that if Jason lost the "Good Day" and continued to earn more Bad Points (up to nine on a weekday or eleven Bad Points on a weekend) he would immediately go to bed. This might occur at 3:00 in the afternoon. Jason would come out for dinner and his bath, but would spend the rest of the day in his bedroom.

The purpose of this rule is to discourage children from abusing the system. Youngsters like Jason are so manipulative that once they lose the "Good Day" star they might act-out for the remainder of the day.

Jason seemed to perk up during the discussion of the Daily Rewards. He suggested food treats, trinkets and television privileges. In addition, he proposed Weekly Rewards of going fishing with his father and going to the park. Jason also wished to go to a baseball trading card store periodically to spend his allowance.

The notions of consistency and consequences, and the idea that rewards were to be earned, not just given, were somewhat foreign to both Cathy and Robert. It was difficult for them to accept that they had to change some of their basic ideas regarding child rearing in order to make a better life for Jason and for themselves. They were somewhat skeptical about the system, but they committed to following through with it.

The family was seen again in two weeks and they brought the Behavior Management chart with them. Jason had performed quite well on the Daily Expectation section, especially on those items that involved the use of a timer.

Cathy noted that he liked to play "beat the buzzer," and was becoming expert at making his bed and getting dressed on time by himself. In fact, Jason was quite proud that he could now brush his teeth without his mother's assistance.

Cathy and Robert were incredulous that Jason could change in terms of his responsibility behavior in such a short time and they were quite pleased with him.

In terms of the Behavior/Attitude Bad Point section, Jason was still evidencing difficulty, especially doing as told the first time without fussing. He had a tendency to have to be asked three times (and to therefore receive three Bad Points, leading to a short Time-Out) before he would be cooperative.

However, in the two week period between appointments he earned ten "Good Days" out of the fourteen. In fact, he had received five "Good Days" out of the previous seven and earned the Weekly Reward of going fishing with his father.

Jason explained very excitedly what he was planning to do for his next Weekly Reward and Cathy and Robert were only too pleased to comply with their youngster's wishes, since he was now behaving appropriately.

Jason's behavior was still not perfect, and Cathy and Robert noted they had allowed several Bad Points to go by without marking them on the chart.

This is a common occurrence when parents begin the system and it often takes several weeks before they adjust their attitude in order to give Bad Points more accurately. They were told that the more strictly they followed the system, the better their son's behavior would be. His behavior was but a barometer of their persistence in using the Behavior Management System.

The family was seen every two weeks for the next two months and gradually the number of Bad Points allowed was decreased so that Jason was allowed only four Bad Points on a school day and six on a weekend. Robert and Cathy did not wish to lower the allowable number below this.

They felt they were being fairly strict with him and that Jason was actually behaving better than most children. They were satisfied with his behavior and although he gave them a run for their money at times, they felt they had adequate control over their son for the first time in many years.

Their home life had calmed down; Jason was going to bed without a fuss; Cathy had more time for herself and their marital relationship had even improved significantly.

In fact, Jason was to visit his grandmother for a week during the summer and the chart was going with him! Robert and Cathy felt his behavior had improved so much that they were certain he would behave for Grandma as long as the chart continued to be employed.

Jason remained on the Behavior Management System for the next six months. After that, the family was able to modify the program so that he was expected to complete "morning chores," "afternoon chores" and "evening chores." This basically included all of the specific chores previously expected but he was now able to have them grouped into three periods of each day.

Jason was now able to handle this broader system and it was easier for Cathy and Robert to keep track of the chart. They felt very comfortable as parents.

During this time, their daughter Kelly was born. They determined that as soon as she was old enough to be responsible for her behavior, she was going to be put on a Behavior Management System also!

Behavior Management for Three through Six-Year-Olds: The "Smiley Face System"

In terms of changing the behavior of noncompliant toddlers and young children, a simplified Behavior Management System referred to as the Smiley Face System is employed.

Parents of young children tend to depend upon threats of spanking, reprimanding and reasoning to alter their youngster's behavior. We often see and hear parents' idle threats in the malls, at grocery stores, in restaurants and in their homes.

Generally, parents have not developed the necessary behavioral style of consistent discipline given in a nonchalant manner in terms of dealing with their young children.

Youngsters can be quite difficult to work with, but it has been found that once limits are set for them, they generally will remain within these boundaries. However, there will be occasional excursions outside of the limits to see how far they can go.

In working with parents of young children, the Smiley Face System for youngsters three through six years of age has been found to be quite effective. These youngsters generally do not have the conceptual ability to understand the Behavior Management System discussed previously and therefore a more simplified model has been developed for younger children.

The Smiley Face System involves three smiley faces drawn on a sheet of paper. One sheet is placed on the front of the refrigerator, using a magnet to hold it and the remainder of the smiley face sheets are placed on top of the refrigerator.

The parent and child are instructed that each time the child behaves inappropriately, the parent will cross out one of the smiley faces. When three smiley faces have been crossed out, consequences will occur to the child.

Inappropriate Behaviors

Inappropriate behaviors for three through six-year-olds generally center around:

- Not doing as told when told

- Aggressiveness

- Touching things without permission

- Interrupting the parent

- Not taking "No" for an answer

- Fussing and throwing temper tantrums

Of course, parents can individualize their program to deal with any inappropriate behavior they wish to decrease.

Consequences

When all three smiley faces have been crossed out, two things will occur. First, the parent will remove one of five treats from a jar that was readied for the child that morning. The items consist of food treats or small, inexpensive trinkets in which the child is interested. The "lost" treat is placed back into the master bag of treats and the child does not have the opportunity to regain that treat that day. Therefore, there are now four treats remaining in the child's jar.

At the same time, the child is then placed in a Time-Out situation. (The reader is encouraged to refer to Time-Out on Page 27.) The length of the Time-Out depends upon the age of the child.

Time-Outs should be at least of five minute duration for three-year-olds and the duration can be raised from ten to fifteen minutes for four, five or six-year-olds.

The Time-Out situation should always be a safe, yet boring place for the child. The purpose of Time-Out is not to harm the youngster, but to be so boring that the child will consider avoiding being placed in Time-Out by behaving more appropriately the next time.

The timer is set for the allotted time and when the child hears it ring, he will know that the parent will only then remove him from the Time-Out situation. If, after coming out of Time-Out the child begins to fuss, the parent will again cross out smiley faces on a new sheet of paper.

This process will be continued throughout the day. That is, the child's behavior is noted on the Smiley Face Chart and each time three smiley faces are crossed off, the child loses one of the five prizes in the jar and also spends an allotted amount of time in Time-Out.

At the end of the day (about one-half hour before the child's bedtime) the youngster receives whatever prizes remain in the jar.

Division of the Day

Very young children (three and four-year-olds) may need to have their day divided into two parts. For instance, they may receive three prizes from wakening until two o'clock and then another three prizes from two o'clock until bedtime. Older children (five and six-year-olds) can usually wait for their rewards until one-half hour before bedtime.

It is suggested that after a long period of time (an hour or two) or a significant break in the day's activities (such as going to the mall or going to nursery school) that a new sheet of smiley faces is applied to the refrigerator.

This prevents the possibility of a youngster having two smiley faces crossed out first thing in the morning, behaving fairly well for the next two hours at the mall and then losing one smiley face after lunch.

This would result in three smiley faces being crossed out. Too much time has intervened and the youngster may not understand why he is being punished.

What To Expect

Children tend to react very intensely to the Smiley Face System. About half of the children perform very well beginning the first day since they appear to be quite attracted to the rewards and they also dislike Time-Out.

Other children (of the more stubborn variety) make a valiant attempt to prove to the parent that the system will not work. They will go into Time-Out and remain there quietly, coming out only to tell the parent they really wanted to be in Time-Out and wouldn't mind returning.

The only appropriate parental reaction would be that of nonchalance. That is, the parent should note to the child that he may earn his way back into the Time-Out room if he likes it so well by misbehaving three more times and having three smiley faces crossed out.

This can be continued throughout the day and often these youngsters are in Time-Out several times a day for the first week. After the first week though, most of these stubborn youngsters begin to tire of the game and really become more interested in earning the rewards. They then recognize that the Time-Out situation is not enjoyable!

Parent/Child Interaction during Time-Out

It is important that the parent not interact with the youngster during Time-Out. Children are not to be given attention during the Time-Out situation. (Again, the reader is referred to Page 27.)

However, the parent must continually listen to the child who is fussing in Time-Out to make sure the fussing is that of anger and not one of being hurt. A hurt child needs to be attended to immediately; an angry child needs to be left to think about the consequences of his behavior.

Effectiveness of the System

This system has been found to be extremely effective if the parent is consistent. This does not mean the parent must cross out a smiley face for every single inappropriate action--only those that are significant.

The children receive the prizes remaining in the jar at the end of the day and the treats are theirs to keep.

They seem to enjoy the rewards, but most children respond well to this system due to dislike of the Time-Out room rather than the rewarding properties of the treats.

Many youngsters need to remain on the Smiley Face System until they are old enough to be placed on the more complex Behavior Management System presented previously.

Some parents feel that they do not wish to have to live such a structured life, but it quickly becomes apparent that without a Behavior Management System of some sort (either the simplified one for youngsters or the more complex one for older children) the home may become chaotic.

Even though Behavior Management Systems can be somewhat time consuming in terms of keeping charts and smiley face forms, the home is run in a much more efficient, calm manner and parents soon find that it is well worth the trouble!

Behavior Management Away From The Home

Parents often ask how to employ Behavior Management Systems when they are outside of the home. Malls and restaurants do not generally provide for effective Time-Out situations. Time-Out can be accomplished to some extent in a corner of a mall but generally it is not as effective as at home in which the child can be placed in a safe, yet boring environment.

It is suggested to parents that they use a golfer's wrist clicker or grocery counter (the type with four knobs) to remind them of how many inappropriate behaviors each child has accumulated while they are out. In this manner, a clicker can be an immediate consequence as well as verification of behavior.

For example, if John behaves inappropriately three times while shopping in the mall with his mother, she will click the counter three times and upon returning home, will cross out three smiley faces on the chart. She will then take away one of his prizes and place him in the Time-Out room.

The parent can also use the clicker by saying to the child, "If you can keep it to two clicks or less while we are in the mall, then I will buy you a drink as we leave."

Another suggestion is to place pennies or nickels in front of a youngster when he is out to dinner. The parent removes one of the five coins when the child acts inappropriately (leaves his seat, talks too loudly, uses bad manners) and the child cannot regain that coin. At the end of the meal, the child receives all of the coins that are left. Usually this is a strong incentive and is a fun way for the child to make it successfully through a dinner experience.

Both parents and children tend to need documentation of the child's behavior. If the parent tries to remember how many inappropriate behaviors each child accumulated while they were on a day trip, it is very difficult and the children will often find ways of sabotaging the system.

If the parent uses a device such as a counter or clicker, there will be no discrepancy. Children are always on the lookout for discrepancies to pull parents off-track and parents must be on guard for this.

In addition, just taking the counter out of the mother's purse can often quiet a child down when he sees that Mom is about to use it!

Sibling Rivalry

Dr. Lynn Clark, in his book entitled, The Time-Out Solution (1989), notes that Time-Out is used very effectively for youngsters who try to engage their parents as "judge or referee" in sibling battles, and that the parent may take "too much responsibility for solving problems between children."

It is often difficult for a parent to determine which child started the argument since both youngsters will most likely blame the other for the disagreement. Very soon the discussion about who started the fuss becomes sidetracked into a full blown argument in and of itself.

The unwitting parent who has become involved in the ruckus is frustrated and the children are more angry than before. Dr. Clark notes that "the children become dependent on parents to settle problems rather than resolving their own problems." (pg. 111).

On the Behavior Management System for older children it was suggested that when siblings fight, both are given a Bad Point, resulting in the potential loss of the Daily Rewards.

67

If the youngsters are under seven years of age, the bickering should result in a smiley face being crossed out, and if it is the third one crossed out, the child will be placed in Time-Out. If both children need to go into Time-Out, one can use the regular Time-Out setting and the other one can use the parents' bedroom or sit in the hall.

Children have been known to sacrifice a Bad Point or a smiley face just to get the other child in trouble. If the parent sees this happening, then the offending child should receive twice as many Bad Points as does the victim child.

Again, it does not pay for the parent to try to be the judge in the children's battles. If one uses Time-Out judiciously with children, giving both of them Bad Points for fighting, eventually the children will tend to feel that it is not worthwhile to fight, especially when the parent is around. They either learn to bicker when the adult is not there, to fight quietly or to separate themselves from each other.

This is exactly what we want from our children. If they can learn self-control by leaving an annoying situation (for example, if someone is being unruly or inappropriate to them) then they have learned a very good lesson in terms of social relationships and self-discipline.

Chapter 4

Academic Achievement: Study Skill Training

> *"When nothing seems to help, I go and look at a stonecutter hammering away at his rock perhaps a hundred times without as much as a crack showing in it. Yet at the hundred and first blow it will split in two, and I know it was not that last blow that did it - but all that had gone before."*
>
> *Jacob Riis*

"My child is not doing as well in school as he can" is one of the most commonly heard concerns of parents today. Whether academic underachievement is based in authority rebellion, laziness or a learning disability, parents should do all that they can to encourage children to work to their innate potential.

Granted, many children are not internally motivated to achieve, and for that matter, neither are many adults. We achieve and perform because of the benefits at the end.

Yes, some individuals work and study for the thrill of success, but this appears to be the exception rather than the rule. Therefore, if the child is not internally motivated but can be encouraged to achieve through external rewards, this should be acceptable as a starting place.

Hopefully, the pride that one achieves from externally motivated academic success will develop strongly enough so that internal needs for academic achievement will follow.

The "Sink or Swim" Philosophy

Too many parents depend upon the "sink or swim" laissez-faire philosophy that encourages youngsters to learn responsibility at their own pace. What psychologists have found is that many of these unmotivated youngsters grow to be equally unmotivated adults, without proper self-controls and educational foundations.

Statistics strongly argue that once a child begins to underachieve and is retained, there is a much greater chance of the child not graduating.

The high school drop-out rate has reached epidemic proportion and is an ever-increasing stress upon our educational system and future human resources.

In fact, a recent State Education Performance Study by the United States Department of Education (1989) showed that in many states well over 30% of high school entrants do not graduate. In other states, over 40% of high school entrants do not graduate!

Effect Upon Society

What does this mean? The obvious effect upon society is that approximately one-third of our young adults will not have an adequate education and will not be able to express themselves properly.

What appears to be even more important is that almost one-third of our young adults will not have the self-control and the self-discipline to remain and perform in a situation that may be uncomfortable or boring to them.

I do not begin to suggest that school should be a pleasant and interesting experience for all individuals. In fact, it is the unique youngster who actually enjoys math class!

However, youngsters need to pay attention and to perform to their potential regardless of whether they enjoy the situation.

The "sink or swim" philosophy of letting children determine whether they will study or not seems to be counter productive for the development of the self-discipline necessary for success in the academic situation and later in life.

The sixth grade retainee of the 1990's may very well be the high school dropout of the next century. Therefore the twenty-first century appears to be arriving with a more than healthy proportion of under-disciplined, disorganized youngsters who are not being properly prepared for the pressures of adult life.

The high school dropout of the 1990's may be the young adult of the twenty-first century who will have great difficulty taking responsibility in terms of employment, marital duties, as well as parenting responsibilities.

The Need for Study Skill Training

Therefore, it is imperative that our youngsters are taught proper study skills and be able to grow up in a home environment that will not tolerate school failure or academic irresponsibility.

Parents must encourage youngsters to achieve to their potential, even if this necessitates strong externally motivated organizational aids.

If the child is not naturally motivated to achieve, parents should provide the child with the opportunities to succeed. Study skill training tactics are often necessary.

When the youngster does "see the light," then he will have the necessary foundation to become an independent learner, to feel good about himself and to beat the odds of academic underachievement.

Michelle

Fifteen year old Michelle was an example of an underachieving child whose parents were distraught and confused by her continued failure in school. Michelle and her parents had come to my office in an effort to understand their daughter's problem.

73

Michelle's sulky expression was complete with poor eye contact, hands stuffed in her pockets and facial expressions ranging from mere boredom to raging annoyance.

Her mother presented a history that was typical of youngsters who underachieve or fail in school. Michelle had performed adequately from kindergarten through fifth grade but she never seemed to actually enjoy school.

Even though Michelle rarely appeared to have homework, her grades had been adequate in the elementary school setting and she had not been a behavior problem.

However, when Michelle entered middle school (which meant changing classes after each subject) things began to fall apart. She rarely seemed to have homework, reporting that she had either completed it in school or the teacher had not assigned any.

She seldom studied for tests and when queried about this, she became so loud and argumentative that her parents began to avoid discussing the subject entirely.

They hoped that Michelle would "see the light" and would begin to study on her own.

This pattern of behavior continued throughout the year and Michelle barely passed the sixth grade. The same pattern occurred in the seventh grade and finally Michelle was retained in the eighth grade.

Her mother again hoped that natural consequences (grade retention) would inspire Michelle and she would become motivated when high school began.

However, the opposite situation actually occurred. Michelle was even more disenchanted than ever with school since she was older than many of her peers and she knew there would be four more long years until she graduated, if ever.

When she began high school, she had already known several of the youngsters, but her prior group of friends seemed to be breaking up. Those who had been good students or belonged to school clubs seemed to go their own ways.

Michelle joined a group of unmotivated, nonachieving youngsters who readily accepted her. These adolescents came to school mainly for social reasons.

Absenteeism and the skipping of classes increased, and Michelle was beginning to become rebellious within the classroom.

The school had begun to consider expulsion, which appeared to be the catalyst that brought Michelle and her parents to my office for evaluation. It quickly became apparent that Michelle and her parents would need assistance with study skill training.

The Basics of Effective Study Skill Training

Study skill training involves teaching the youngster organizational skills which, if internalized, will last a lifetime.

If these skills can be learned as children, they will be able to utilize effective strategies in the work and home environments as adults.

The four parts of study skill training involve:

- A parent/teacher/child conference to set up the Daily Report Card System

- Establishing criteria for a "Good Day" on the Daily Report Card

- Setting up consequences (both positive and negative) for academic behavior as evidenced on the Daily Report Card

- The use of the Study Buddy System

I have found that consistent usage of all four components always leads to better grades and to a greater retention of the material presented.

In addition, most youngsters who complete the program become internally motivated to achieve in school, which in turn greatly heightens their self-esteem.

The Daily Report Card System

The Daily Report Card follows on Page 78. Column A lists the child's subjects (in order) above the dotted line and allows for the teacher's signature below the line.

Column B provides a space for the listing of Homework and Incomplete Classwork (to be completed later as homework).

Column C addresses long-term projects such as book reports, tests or projects to be completed.

Column D offers a space for the teacher to check whether the student has turned in the previous day's homework (Yes, No or N/A-not applicable).

Columns E and F deal with Satisfactory or Unsatisfactory class work and class behavior, respectively.

Column G presents a weekly notice of any homework assignments missed and any test/quiz grades obtained by the child that week.

Setting up the Daily Report Card

A school conference with the child, parent(s) and teacher(s) is mandatory for successful modification of a youngster's inappropriate school habits.

The parent supplies several copies of the Daily Report Card form that is described to the child and teachers at the school conference. A new Daily Report Card sheet is to be used each day.

DAILY REPORT CARD

Date_____   Name:_____

A Subject/Teacher's Signature	B Homework/Class-work Incomplete	C Book Reports/Tests/Projects Announced	D Homework Turned In			E Class Work		F Class Behavior		G Friday Report
			Yes	No	N/A	S	U	S	U	
	None ( ) Due ( )	Date: Topic: None ( )								Homework Assign missed Test Grades
	None ( ) Due ( )	Date: Topic: None ( )								Homework Assign missed Test Grades
	None ( ) Due ( )	Date: Topic: None ( )								Homework Assign missed Test Grades
	None ( ) Due ( )	Date: Topic: None ( )								Homework Assign missed Test Grades
	None ( ) Due ( )	Date: Topic: None ( )								Homework Assign missed Test Grades
	None ( ) Due ( )	Date: Topic: None ( )								Homework Assign missed Test Grades
	None ( ) Due ( )	Date: Topic: None ( )								Homework Assign missed Test Grades
	None ( ) Due ( )	Date: Topic: None ( )								Homework Assign missed Test Grades

78

During Michelle's school conference it was noted that at the end of each period she was to write down what homework, if any, had been announced that day by the teacher (Column B). If there were no assignments announced, she was to check on the form noting that no homework was due.

Next she was to note if there were any projects, book reports or tests announced. She was to write down the topic and the date due, if any, in Column C. If none were announced, Michelle was to check "None" on the form.

The next section indicated whether Michelle had turned in the prior day's homework, which was to be checked by the teacher and noted in Column D.

The teacher was to check how much effort Michelle had produced that day (Column E) and to note how her behavior had been in class (Column F.)

At the end of each class, Michelle was to give her Daily Report Card to the teacher to be validated by signature in Column A verifying accuracy and then put the form in her folder for use in her next class.

At the end of each day, she was to use the Daily Report Card as a guide to assessing the materials she was to take home in order to complete her homework.

Each Friday, the teachers were also to note the number of homework assignments not turned in, if any, and any quiz/test grades obtained that week in Column G.

(If a child does not have trouble turning in completed homework or has no behavior problems in the class-room, the parent may wish to consider using the Simplified Daily Report Card, an example of which is given on Page 81.)

Criteria and Consequences: Achieving a "Good Day" on the Daily Report Card System

This section is an especially important portion of study skill training in that it must be very clear to the child what must be accomplished to achieve a "Good Day" on the Daily Report Card. I instructed Michelle and her mother that if she:

- filled out the Daily Report Card appropriately;

- obtained all of the teachers' signatures;

- brought home all of the necessary homework materials, and

- received four or less unsatisfactory marks each day regarding her class effort and class behavior

she would have achieved a "Good Day" on the Daily Report Card.

For a "Good Day" she would receive one dollar plus a certain amount of "credit" toward buying new clothes (for example, a poker chip worth one dollar toward a

SIMPLIFIED DAILY REPORT CARD

Date_____   Name:_____

A	B	C	D
Subject/Teacher's Signature	Homework/Class-work Incomplete	Book Reports/Tests/ Projects Announced	Friday Report
	None ( ) Due ( )	Date: Topic: None ( )	Homework Assign missed Test Grades
	None ( ) Due ( )	Date: Topic: None ( )	Homework Assign missed Test Grades
	None ( ) Due ( )	Date: Topic: None ( )	Homework Assign missed Test Grades
	None ( ) Due ( )	Date: Topic: None ( )	Homework Assign missed Test Grades
	None ( ) Due ( )	Date: Topic: None ( )	Homework Assign missed Test Grades
	None ( ) Due ( )	Date: Topic: None ( )	Homework Assign missed Test Grades
	None ( ) Due ( )	Date: Topic: None ( )	Homework Assign missed Test Grades
	None ( ) Due ( )	Date: Topic: None ( )	Homework Assign missed Test Grades

clothing purchase of her choice when she had accumulated enough poker chips). She would also be allowed her usual privileges regarding socializing and use of the telephone, TV, stereo, etc.

If she didn't accomplish all of these criteria, she would remain in a Time-Out situation for a specified period when she came home from school. She also would not receive any of the rewards since a "Good Day" had not been achieved.

Time-Out

An appropriate Time-Out situation for an adolescent is to have the youngster spend thirty to sixty minutes in a boring, yet safe, environment. A child's bedroom is often not boring, so the parent is cautioned against using this for Time-Out. The child may sit in a bathroom, a guest room or perhaps even the parent's bedroom for the allotted amount of Time-Out.

Michelle was incredulous that I would suggest that her mother take away all of her recreational time (going out with her friends, watching television, talking on the telephone and listening to her stereo). To top it off, she was even more angry when I suggested placing her in a Time-Out situation! She even threatened that she would not go into the Time-Out room.

I dealt with her refusal by noting that if she did not go into Time-Out she would not be allowed to go out the following weekend. That seemed to capture Michelle's attention since she lived for Friday and Saturday evenings!

It became obvious that, at least initially, Michelle would respond to the negative consequences rather than the positive ones. It is not uncommon for youngsters to be more attuned to avoiding negative consequences rather than gaining rewards at the beginning of the Daily Report Card System.

The Study Buddy System

In the meantime, I had already set up a "Study Buddy" for Michelle. A Study Buddy is a high school-aged youngster who enjoys tutoring others who are not progressing to their ability. Study Buddies can be found via the local high school guidance office or through the teacher/sponsor of the school's National Honor Society.

They must provide their own transportation to the child's home and generally earn $4.50 an hour tutoring the youngster. This is a small price to pay when one considers that the parent/child relationship is at stake during homework confrontations. In addition, youngsters usually enjoy working with a Study Buddy whereas they dread working with their parents.

Setting up the System

Michelle's Study Buddy, Eric, came to her home Monday through Thursday for an hour and one-half to two hours each day to help her with her homework and to prepare for tests and projects. This is not to say that Eric was doing Michelle's homework, but that he was encouraging Michelle as well as guiding her when necessary.

He would teach her how to break down her assignments so that long-term projects were dealt with over several days, not hurriedly attempted the night before they were due. Psychologists have long known that "distributed practice" leads to much greater retention than does "massed practice." In other words, cramming doesn't work!

Eric divided the assignments so that Michelle was able to study a small part each day. When it came time to review for the entire test, she therefore already had a strong foundation. They used a calendar to note when each long-range assignment was due by marking the date each day until the project was to be completed.

This helped remind both Eric and Michelle to continue to work on long-range projects and not just on assignments due the next day.

The Course of Events

I saw Michelle and her mother two weeks after they had started the Daily Report Card System and the Study Buddy had begun working with her.

She had a slow start in that it was difficult for her to remember to obtain the teachers' signatures on the Daily Report Card at the end of each period.

However, the third day she had acquired five out of the six teacher signatures and had obtained all of them by the fourth day!

She tried to hide the fact that she was somewhat pleased with herself. She still felt that the system was unnecessary and was only doing it to prevent losing her daily and weekend privileges.

Her work with the Study Buddy was exceptional. Michelle worked very well with Eric, most likely to avoid a hassle with someone of her own age.

She did not want to appear selfish, demanding and childish to Eric and therefore paid attention and worked well with him.

In fact, Eric and Michelle were becoming friends and between work sessions they began to compare notes on acquaintances and activities.

(This is a common result of the Study Buddy/student relationship and in the many cases in which I have linked a Study Buddy with a youngster, no one has failed to achieve success!)

Michelle's Success

I followed Michelle weekly for the next several months and even had Eric come to my office periodically for a session with her. It was not always a perfect situation and Michelle experienced Time-Out occasionally, but the impact on her attitude toward school and her production of homework was tremendous.

By the end of the next grading period, Michelle had raised her grades from "F's" and "D's" to "C's" and "B's."

She would not directly express pride in her accomplishments, but one could see in her demeanor that she was, indeed, happier with herself.

This previously sulky, belligerent and controlling youngster had begun to become internally motivated to perform in school.

It would still take many more months of intensive usage of the Daily Report Card and the Study Buddy systems for Michelle to become an independent learner. In fact, many youngsters do not reach the independent status of internal motivation for several years, but when it happens, it is endlessly gratifying to everyone concerned.

Michelle was one of the lucky ones. She now had a chance to grow to her potential as an adult. But she is just one of the large population of unmotivated preteens and adolescents who are not prepared via effective study skills for the unstructured situations that they face at the middle and high school levels.

Therefore, parents must structure school responsibilities for them. This is not to say that every youngster needs training in structuring and organizational tactics, because many have already developed these skills either on their own or through parental guidance.

However, those who are not internally motivated to perform and who do not have effective study skills must be trained by at least the sixth grade year how to tackle the academic environment in an efficient manner.

Grade School Daily Report Card System for Kindergarten Through 5th Grade Students

Youngsters in the elementary school setting generally do not change classes; at the most they have a morning teacher and an afternoon teacher.

The Grade School Daily Report Card seen on Page 88 notes several areas of difficulty that children tend to display in the classroom. These include difficulties in terms of completing classwork, following directions, getting right down to work, talking out of turn or making noises.

If the child is having difficulty in these or other areas, a school conference is called and the teachers are asked to make a small "x" in each column which addresses behavior problem areas.

For example, if the child talks out of turn six times in the morning, there would be six "x's" next to that item in the morning teacher's column.

In addition, after the child has written what homework is due and any projects or book reports announced (this is specified on the right side of the form) then the teacher signs the Grade School Daily Report Card.

The teacher's signature validates that what the child has written for homework, projects, book reports and tests is accurate, so that the parent has a complete idea each day of what is due. There is also a place for teacher comments, if necessary.

Grade School Daily Report Card

Student _____ Teacher's Signature _____ x = Problem in this area

Date _____ Teacher's Signature _____ _____ total points received

Problem Areas	A.M.	P.M.	Assignments
1. Completes classwork			Homework and Incomplete Classwork
2. Follows directions			
3. Gets right down to work			
4. Pays attention to teacher			
5. Tries hard to do assignments			Date due:
6. Respects the rights of others (keeps hands to self) (doesn't disturb others)			Projects, Book Reports, Tests Announced
7. Follows class and school rules			
8. Does not talk out of turn Does not make rude noises			Date Due:
9. Attitude and behavior is acceptable in special classes (art, music, physical ed., etc.)			Teacher's Comments:
10. Stays in seat			

88

The Grade School Daily Report Card is placed in a file folder and kept at the child's desk so that the teacher makes a notation on it as the problem behaviors occur during the day.

In this way the child knows exactly how many points he or she has at the moment. The parent and teachers decide how many points the child is allowed in order to have a "Good Day" at school.

If the child keeps the number of points ("x's") to that maximum or less, then the youngster receives a reward after school. Rewards such as a soft drink at a local convenience store or a poker chip worth a certain amount toward a prize given during the next weekend are typical treats.

If the child exceeds the number of points allowed, then he loses the daily prize and also faces a negative consequence such as Time-Out or not being able to watch television for the remainder of the day.

If the parent, teacher and child employ this form diligently, the parent knows each day how the child performed and also what is due the next day in terms of homework or studying for tests.

This gives the parent an accurate indication of how the child is performing on a daily basis and in which areas the child needs improvement.

If the youngster does not bring the Grade School Daily Report Card home, then the parent is to assume that it was a "Bad Day." Therefore the child would automatically not receive the reward and would be negatively consequated. This rule helps to deter the child from losing the report.

The Grade School Daily Report Card form is quite useful and helps the child to learn self-control within the classroom. In addition, the youngster will become more organized in terms of dealing with homework assignments, projects and tests.

Use of this System

Most youngsters will benefit from the Daily Report Card System. Many will need teacher signatures to insure that assignments are accurate, whereas other more attentive children can be allowed to document daily assignments without teacher validation. However, a Daily Report Card or daily assignment sheet is the core of Study Skill Training.

Although many youngsters can complete their assignments without the aid of a Study Buddy, those who have a history of non-completion of work will benefit greatly from this guidance.

Often parents ask if a Study Skill Training Program (Daily Report Card and Study Buddy System) can be set up at the same time as a Behavior Management System for the home. It is recommended that the academic situation generally be modified first and then once that is under control, the Home Behavior Management System can be initiated.

Chapter 5

Issues of Development

> *I have found the best way to give advice to your children is to first ask what they want and then advise them to do it.*
>
> *Harry S. Truman*

As children grow and develop, we see constant changes in personality, likes and dislikes, and techniques of dealing with frustration.

This Chapter addresses the specific developmental issues of phases of childhood manipulation, pre-adolescent moodiness and the adult child who refuses to grow up.

Phases of Manipulation

It's two o'clock in the morning and nine-month-old Kary is awake and crying. Her mother wakes up, hovering between sleep and consciousness, hoping that the discomfort is temporary and the baby will soon fall asleep again.

After three or four grueling minutes mother gives in, takes the baby into her bed and watches Kary happily cuddle up and fall asleep.

Exhausted, as this has become a nightly pattern, Kary's mother tries not to be angry and to fall asleep herself.

However, her emotions take over and she resentfully wonders how she has allowed this tiny creature to disturb her own sleep habits and therefore leave her exhausted day after day. Could this lovely, innocent nine-month-old actually be controlling her mother?

Four-year-old Sean, who is normally somewhat active, becomes a guided missile as he careens through racks of clothes at the department store.

At home Sean is strong-willed, but seems to abide by the rules of the house since he knows that he will be sent to his room if he becomes too rough.

However, in the unstructured environment of a mall or store, he seems to lose control and all parental threats appear to fall upon deaf ears. The tyke runs away from his mother, tugs on racks of clothes and uses the clothing turntable as a playhouse.

How could this child who is manageable at home lose control so easily when at the department store? Could he actually realize, at the tender age of four years, that his mother's repertoire of consequences is limited outside of the home and therefore perceives the situation as a free-for-all?

Or, consider ten-year-old Michael. Michael has recently begun to look depressed, expressing feelings of social rejection and often forlornly questions what the family would feel like if he had never been born.

Instantaneous guilt pangs rush through his parents' minds as they wonder if he is contemplating running away or even worse, harming himself. After discussing the situation with each other, the parents note a pattern to Michael's behavior.

He seems to look depressed and mentions not being part of the family only after being reprimanded for a misdeed or when his requests are not immediately granted. Could a youngster of ten years actually be manipulating his parents' guilt feelings?

Psychologists have studied phases of children's manipulatory behavior for decades. Several interesting patterns have emerged. Babies as young as three months of age understand cause and effect relationships, and therefore have the basic tools for budding manipulatory behavior.

In addition, as children mature and cognitive ability develops, the nature of child manipulatory tactics becomes more complex, organized and planful. In other words, unsuspecting parents can become victims of manipulatory behavior of tyrannical tykes without even realizing it!

As children mature, the techniques of manipulation become more sophisticated. This is based in the cognitive and emotional development of the youngster.

Babies are quite reflexive; they feel urges that need to be satisfied and their responses are limited to crying, smiling, fussing and babbling.

Very early in their lives babies learn that adults respond in a predictable fashion. A smile elicits a hug and a smile in return, a giggle elicits a parental laugh, and most importantly, a scream merits instantaneous parental attention.

This cause/effect relationship does not go unnoticed by the four-month-old. She is learning more each day what effect her behavior has upon the world around her.

Kary, for instance, had been inadvertently trained by her mother to cry loudly when she woke up during the night. The baby had learned that crying led to being removed from the crib and to being placed in the warmth of the parental bed.

Kary had no cognition of the negative effects that her behavior had on her mother's life--all she realized was that crying led to cuddling. Crying, in an evolutionary sense, has been a necessity, since the helpless infant's cry alerts the parent to the youngster's needs.

However, many parents do not make the discrimination between coming to the aid of a needy child and falling prey to a manipulative youngster.

The cause/effect relationship described above was not coincidental. The baby's cognitive development was sophisticated and allowed her to determine that crying elicited immediate attention. As long as her mother continued to react predictably, Kary would continue to awaken and cry during the night.

By the age of four years, the youngster's cognition is even more highly developed. Four-year-olds can predict consequences, can delay immediate gratification of their needs and can selectively control their behavior depending upon the situation.

It is not unusual to hear of a preschooler who behaves appropriately for his teacher but runs his parents ragged at home. The difference lies in the environment.

Preschoolers can select their behavior adeptly--controlling themselves in situations where consequences are clear (for instance, at school) and acting-out at home if limits are not clearly provided or if the boundaries change daily.

Sean exemplifies the typical four-year-old who is already a professional at manipulating his mother. He can select what behaviors he can get away with depending upon the situation.

At home, he knows that his mother will utilize one or more of several punishments for inappropriate behavior. He has experienced spankings, Time-Out in his bedroom, as well as the removal of television privileges.

However, Sean realizes that his mother's attention is easily diverted in a store environment. He knows that he can wander, get into things and that her bag of parental tricks is limited when away from home, so he grabs the opportunity to act-out when the consequences for his inappropriate behavior are unclear.

Parents should never underestimate the creative manipulatory behavior of even a toddler. The trick is to "outmanipulate the manipulator" and to not fall prey to incredibly persistent controlling tactics which youngsters possess.

This becomes an even more difficult task as the child grows to his preteen years. Cognitive development has matured to the point that the ten or eleven-year-old can organize and plan his manipulatory attack.

If the youngster also has budding dramatic skills--watch out! The parent is certain prey for this youngster as he goes in for the kill.

Typical manipulatory techniques for this age child involve threats of running away, subtle hints of harming one's self and references to feeling socially rejected. Badgering, intimidation, threats and martyrdom are also common manipulatory tactics.

Remember Michael, the ten-year-old who realized that expressing feelings of social rejection generally resulted in parental guilt feelings as well as parental attention?

Michael is a manipulatory champ. He can knock the wind out of a parent with a single comment. Michael's behavior presents the common manipulatory tactic of using emotional instability or feelings of sadness.

Children quickly perceive their parents' hot buttons and guilt provocation is a classic example. The parent who perceives his child as sad or depressed can be easily overwhelmed by the child's displayed emotion and the parent can actually feel responsible for the youngster's negative self-concept.

The child who employs this maneuver is especially cagey, as he keeps his parents on edge, not wanting to upset the youngster.

It is important, therefore, that parents learn to understand and to deal effectively with childhood manipulatory behavior. If the parent does not tackle controlling techniques directly, the youngster will grab the reins of power as the parent abdicates control to the child.

Youngsters who are in control of the family are often lacking in self-control themselves, leading to a chaotic situation. Dealing effectively with the developmental stages of childhood manipulation involves three basic processes:

1. It is imperative that parents understand the incredible length that children will go to in employing control tactics. Controlling behavior is normal behavior, although some children are more manipulative than others.

    What often appears as reflexive behavior (crying, pouting, negative self-statements) is, upon careful examination, seen to be planned manipulatory reaction. The parent who does not realize that youngsters and even babies can control their emotions and behaviors is in for a rude awakening!

    One must constantly be on the alert for signs of childhood manipulation. Negative patterns and habits are often behaviors which have been reinforced or rewarded inadvertently. In other words, children behave due to the consequences of their actions.

If fussing, crying or threatening results in gaining a goal, children will continue to behave in this manner in the future.

This is an insidious process. Parents are usually unaware of the intense effect that giving in to a manipulatory tactic has upon a child.

When a youngster is fussing and the parent placates the child in an effort to quiet him, the parent has inadvertently taught the youngster that disruptive behavior will lead to gratification of one's demands. In the short run this philosophy appears to be effective--the child temporarily is satisfied and quiets down.

However, the long-term effects upon the child are disastrous. The youngster is actually being educated to be manipulative in order to have his needs met.

2. Parents need to become adept at employing "*awfulization.*" This is the process of considering the worst case scenario of behaviors that children of various developmental stages can produce.

    Often parents find that the child's actual manipulatory behavior is much less intimidating than the *awfulized* assumption.

If the parent realizes, for instance, that the worst thing that a baby can do is to scream, one can put this into better perspective. A screaming child has never actually harmed an adult. If the parent behaves appropriately, the screaming will cease.

Too many parents dread their child's screaming and will do anything to stop it. In addition, many parents feel that their child may cease to love them if the youngster is punished for negative behavior.

In reality, the child will cease to respect the parent if he is not given appropriate consequences for his inappropriate behavior.

The worst things that preschoolers can do is to hit, kick, yell "I hate you," have a temper tantrum or misbehave in public. This can be quite embarrassing, especially in the middle of a department store.

While their child is tantruming, parents may feel that everyone is looking at them, waiting to see what they will do. Often parents feel helpless in this situation, at the mercy of their youngster's disruptive behavior.

Again, if the parent has learned to implement consequences for inappropriate behavior, the situation can be effectively handled.

Awfulizing about the possibilities of the older child or pre-teen can be a traumatic process. Fears of youngsters running away, using drugs or capricious mood swings are quite common for parents of this age child.

Guilt provocation is perhaps the most effective manipulatory tactic that a child can employ at this age. The unsuspecting parent may find herself tangled in a web of feeling responsible for her child's actions or self-concept.

This can be paralyzing as the parent fears that any action taken may push the child into "one of her moods."

Again, appropriate consequences can diffuse the situation if the parent is perceptive and realizes that he or she is "being had."

3. Setting up effective boundaries and guidelines for the youngster so that the child will clearly understand what the rules of behavior are is imperative.

In addition, consistent consequences for inappropriate behavior need to be established.

Infants and Toddlers

How does one set up consequences for manipulatory behavior? The technique is dependent upon the child's stage of development. Baby's crying and fussing behaviors should not be catered to automatically.

Once the parent determines that the child is not actually in distress but is relying on a habitual pattern (for instance, that of waking up at night) the parent should not reinforce the crying behavior.

Kary's mother should change her wet diaper, talk to her in a soothing manner and place her back in her crib. Kary's response will most likely be to cry even louder and the howling may last for well over an hour.

Usually, the baby will tire of the fuss and will fall back to sleep. However, Kary will try again the next night and for several nights after that.

If her parents are consistent, she will learn that howling will not lead to the parental bed and she will stop this behavior. Most likely she will also cease waking early in the morning since the waking habit is no longer being reinforced.

When parents are told to "bite the bullet" and refrain from giving in to a crying baby, it is obviously a very traumatic suggestion. However, the end result is so rewarding that it is well worth the week of agonizing nights as the baby cries herself to sleep.

Young Children

Preschool age and older children's manipulatory behavior is best dealt with through a Behavior Management System. The Smiley Face System has been found to be quite effective for younger children (See page 59).

Manipulatory behaviors generally center around not doing as told when told, aggressiveness, touching things without permission, tantruming behavior and not taking "No" for an answer.

If Sean loses three smiley faces while shopping in the mall with his mother, she will click the counter three times and, upon returning home, will cross out three smiley faces on the chart.

She will then take away one of his prizes and place him in the Time-Out room.

Spankings can also be effective with the young child, but only in certain circumstances. In most cases a small swat to the child's hind quarters can gain his attention and may stop the problematical behavior temporarily.

Some children respond well to the threat of spanking, but again, this is the exception rather than the rule. It is inappropriate to spank a child so hard that it brings a welt to the targeted area, since this usually occurs when the parent is very angry and the child could easily become harmed.

Parents have noted that they have spanked the child even while they were well-controlled. However, the youngster may have moved suddenly and the swat that was meant for the child's arm actually hit the child in the mouth, causing a cut lip.

Most parents spank due to anger and they do not particularly aim their swats. Therefore, what generally results from swatting is either a child who has not learned anything positive from the incident or a child who is actually physically hurt by the spanking.

In the latter case, this results not only in physical harm, but anger and distrust for the parent. A parent who spanks is a poor role model for the child. Spankings can teach the youngster that physical aggression is an appropriate way of handling problems.

The parent who aggresses against his child may produce a youngster who aggresses against his peers.

The Older Child

Dealing with the manipulatory behavior of the older child or pre-teen can be even more complex than what is necessary for younger children. During this age, children understand perfectly well what their limits are if the parents set boundaries for them. Limits should follow the "four C's." They must be *Concise, Clear, Consistent,* and at times consequences should be *Catastrophic.*

Concise and clear limits are mandatory in terms of rule-setting. Children have a way of finding loopholes in rules if the limits are not clearly established and concisely presented.

The youngster who has been told not to overfeed the fish in the morning may feed the fish too much in the evening. His indignant retort to the parent who wishes to punish the child may be, "You told me not to overfeed the fish in the morning, but you didn't say anything about overfeeding them in the evening!"

Parents can become easily exasperated by this type of manipulation and loophole finding, and must, therefore, establish rules in broad and encompassing terms such as, "Never overfeed the fish!"

Children can be like human calculators when keeping mental track of parental inconsistencies. Consequences for inappropriate behaviors must be applied consistently.

For example, the child may note, "You didn't punish me yesterday for bugging my brother, and now it's unfair to send me to my room today for hitting him."

The child does have a point. The parent is sending mixed messages and the child will use this to his perceived advantage.

The last "C" involves catastrophic consequences. The most effective consequence has been found to be Time-Out, since it can usually be initiated immediately and it generally attracts a child's attention.

Children hate boredom and they love attention. They would much rather be spanked, reprimanded or have a toy taken away than to be placed in Time-Out. In fact, youngsters will often try to bargain with parents to negotiate loss of possessions rather than being placed in a Time-Out situation.

Outmanipulating the manipulator can be a trying task, and the first step is the perception that even very young children can select their emotions and behaviors by the reaction they wish to receive from the adult.

Once the notion of child manipulation is accepted, the parent can then become a more effective disciplinarian and not fall prey to children's controlling tactics.

More importantly, youngsters need to learn alternative methods of meeting their needs. Problem solving techniques should be addressed with youngsters as alternatives to manipulation.

Pre-Adolescent Moodiness

You may have been one of the lucky minority to have given birth to and raised a delightful, compliant youngster who has been a joy throughout the first nine years.

These youngsters tend to be reasonable, have an active conscience and usually will respond to parental desires and requests readily.

Children who are compliant do have their off days but generally the parent can count on the child to be reasonable and to understand the necessity for discipline and changes in plans.

These reasonable youngsters are emotionally stable and go with the flow quite readily. However, guidelines, structure and limit setting are helpful even with these easy children since boundaries define life to them in a clear fashion.

Compliant youngsters tend to enjoy and do very well on Behavior Management Systems. Often the compliant child is placed on this system due to the need for Behavior Management for a noncompliant sibling. When all children in a family are placed on the Behavior Management System it seems to work better than when the targeted noncompliant child is on the system alone.

Reasonable children take great pleasure in achievement and success and the daily notation of a Good Day on the Behavior Management System is enjoyed tremendously. However, the hands of time do move, and when your delightful nine-year-old turns ten, you may witness an unusual phenomenon occurring before your very eyes.

Within a few months after her tenth birthday you may see a somewhat different child! Although she is still the same good natured, reasonable youngster, one may see the "ten-year-old moodies" emerging.

The beautiful butterfly may turn into a chameleon. Chameleon children change color (or rather mood) depending upon the foliage (the peer group). With quiet, docile, compliant friends, the child acts as one of the group: quiet and compliant.

When the ten-year-old is with twelve and thirteen-year-olds, she acts as one of their group: moody, inconsistent and into the latest fads!

This change may be based in premenstrual physiology for the female, or the child may simply be growing up and becoming overwhelmed with the decisions of whether to act like a preteen or to remain as a child.

A similar metamorphosis occurs with boys, but it appears a few years later. When the change happens, the parent is forewarned that this previously reasonable youngster may now have more frequent emotional outbursts, which are best described as moodiness.

Moodiness is exemplified by the child's ability to turn a normal parental comment into a situation of feeling criticized and persecuted. Ten-year-olds tend to feel very defensive when criticized.

This stage is not obvious in chronically noncompliant youngsters. They have been like that all of their life and this behavior is not new to the parent.

However, when a previously delightful child enters this stage, the parent is shocked by the display of a personality characteristic previously unseen or undeveloped.

What is occurring is that the ten-year-old is no longer a docile, compliant little girl but is a generally compliant preteen who has quite a few decisions to make regarding her behavior.

She is now faced with significant peer pressure as to whether to behave or not. There is a great deal of stress upon her to perceive things in a way different than her parent may wish her to perceive them. She is growing up, gaining some rebellious attitudes and perhaps feeling her oats.

During this time period, it is extremely important for parents not to overreact to the Jekyll and Hyde personality who now lives with them. This is a very natural stage of development for the youngster and the parent should also view it as normal.

The most effective parental attitude in response to ten-year-old mood swings is to remember the good times and to always keep in mind that the child is basically a caring, sensitive youngster who is really not out to get the parent. She is merely exploring alternative ways of dealing with new feelings and perceiving the world in a different manner than before.

Therefore, it is helpful that the parent spends a great deal of time with the youngster during this stage of development. If this is not carried out properly, the youngster most likely will not want to spend any time with the parent when she is thirteen years of age.

Therefore, ages ten through twelve are a time when the parent needs to have quality, one-to-one time with the youngster on a consistent basis. Weekly trips with the child for ice cream or perhaps going for a drive (without other siblings) usually presents a good opportunity to keep the parent/child bond flourishing.

At first the youngster may not wish to talk about anything personal but may chose to use this time to complain about siblings and how unfair things are. In addition, there may be a great deal of talk about how other children do not like your son or daughter.

Reflective responding (or active listening) on the part of the parent (i.e., "I could see how that would upset you") is quite effective in these situations.

The child is not really looking for answers at this age, especially since there are none to give when it comes to dealing with pre-adolescent self-perceptions that change hourly. Most children go through stages of feeling that nobody likes them.

The child needs to feel that the parent cares, understands and is willing to take the time to listen to the youngster. Reflecting the child's concerns solves all three of these necessities.

The child will feel that the parent is taking the time to listen to her concerns and although the parent is not giving advice, the youngster knows that the parent cares.

In addition, the child does not really want advice. Giving parental suggestions will probably only annoy the youngster. Any advice that parents could offer would most likely receive a "yes, but" or a "what if . . ." response.

The preteen does not want answers. She just wants to blow off steam and know that someone cares and perhaps has experienced similar feelings in their own childhood.

Youngsters who can establish or re-establish their relationship with the parent during this developmental stage respond to parents more favorably in their teenage years. They view the parent as trustworthy and able to listen to the child's concerns without overreacting.

Teenagers who cannot trust their parents go to their friends for help and as may be expected, other teenagers may not offer the best advice or alternatives.

If the preteen can learn to trust the parent in terms of displaying good listening skills and having a calm attitude when suggestions are made that may be counter to the adult's predilections, the youngster will develop into a teenager who will address concerns with the parent first.

When the parent of the reasonable child begins to see ten-year-old moodiness emerge she should not despair! This is a natural phenomenon and can be managed by giving the youngster more quality time, active listening and reflection (rather than advice and lecturing).

Children Who Are Hesitant to Grow Up

The adult child who remains at home is somewhat of an enigma. As was noted in earlier chapters, the sink or swim philosophy is generally not the appropriate parenting technique for use with the young child or the adolescent.

Parents must become involved with their children's problematical behaviors and often must force situations upon their youngsters, such as the Study Buddy and the Daily Report Card Systems.

However, the unmotivated young adult no longer fits into this category. These individuals are often beyond the need for parental structure and they should be encouraged to live on their own in an independent manner.

Our society has changed drastically in the past fifty years. When America was a chiefly agrarian society parents often had large families in order to have children to work the fields. In addition, the children tended to marry quite early (often at thirteen or fourteen years of age) and to begin to have children of their own.

Since then, technology has changed the fabric of American life and many families have decided to have only one or two children. Today's youngsters tend to reach adulthood but not act as maturely as their predecessors of the 1920's or 1930's.

It is not unusual to see adult children of twenty-two and twenty-three years of age still living at home. In some families this is seen as an annoyance but other parents actually prefer this arrangement.

There are cases of adult children living at home where the parents feel that the individual is not mature enough to go away to college and rightly so. Therefore they will encourage the child to stay at home to attend a junior college.

This allows the adult child two more years at home in a structured situation where he can gain greater independence under the watchful eye of the parent. Often this is a successful plan and the youngster can then continue with the remainder of the four-year program at a residential college with greater confidence and more organizational strategies under his belt.

In another case, the youngster who is not ready at twenty-two years of age to leave home may not be ready at thirty years of age to leave home either! This is the type of youngster focused upon throughout this book in terms of not having developed self-control and the ability to make appropriate judgments. This individual will remain at home as long as the parent will tolerate.

Often these adult children are quite irresponsible and do not manage money well. Parents feel guilty asking them to leave the home because they perceive that the child will not be able to take care of himself.

These youngsters are chronic excuse makers. They usually have a reason for not being independent and generally they blame their behavior on their parents.

Excuses range from the perception that the parents should have put them in private school rather than public school, or that they had a series of poor teachers, or that their sibling received more attention than they did.

However, all of these are rationalizations and the irresponsible adult child epitomizes the end result of growing up with a lack of self-control.

These individuals will continue to act in an irresponsible manner if their parents do not take control and encourage them to go out on their own.

This is, indeed, a very difficult situation. Parents may feel guilty because they tend to take the responsibility for the adult child not having developed self-control and responsibility. They feel that they would be "throwing the child to the wolves" if the adult youngster left the home prematurely.

However, children who feel that they can remain at home endlessly often will not do the preparatory work necessary for leaving home. When they know that there is a warm bed and three meals a day at home they may complain about having to live with their parents, but they are often manipulative individuals, realizing that the home situation is much easier than being out on their own.

Counselors generally suggest to the parents of this type of adult child to give them fair warning, such as three months notice, that they will have to move out on a certain date. The parents should give them enough money to tide them over for the first month.

If the adult child fails to make further plans for support, the parents should not help out financially beyond the initial subsidy. If the adult child does not take the parents seriously, it is going to be a very rude awakening when the parent follows through with the plan.

The parents need to stand firm (even in the face of tremendous guilt feelings) because giving in to the adult child only confirms his perception that the parents did not actually mean what they said.

In this case the parent is being held hostage and the adult child may feel as if he has won, but he has actually lost in the long run.

Irresponsible adult children have difficulty learning to be on their own and when the parents can no longer be of help (either through illness or death) these individuals are ill prepared for independent living.

Many facilities have been developed for helping this type of adult child begin to live an independent life. Halfway houses and vocational/technical schools have been very helpful.

It should be noted that the adult child may harbor ill feelings toward the parents, as well as the feeling of being rejected. However, this is a small price to pay when it comes to the adult child's long-term ability to live on his own in an independent fashion.

It is never too late to learn self-control, although it is more difficult to learn as an adult. Adult children need to learn self-control in small doses.

They need to learn how to deal with financial matters such as checkbooks and budgeting, vocational issues and eventual marital plans. Psychological guidance can be quite helpful to the hesitant adult child as he or she is forced to leave the womb!

There is always the case of the youngster who, no matter how much one tries to help him, chooses not to be responsible for himself. The parents of such a child have to make the difficult decision of whether to "kick the child out and let him sink or swim" or let him live at home for the rest of their lives. This is a rare case, but of great concern to the parents who have to deal with this type of irresponsible person.

The parent should receive counseling from a therapist to either gain the courage to force the child to leave or to gain the patience to allow the child to stay.

Chapter 6

The Child With Attention Deficit Disorder

Parents were invented to make children happy by giving them something to ignore.

Ogden Nash

Throughout this book the issues of self-discipline and compliance have been addressed for both the home and school environments. Behavior Management Programs and the Daily Report Card/Study Buddy Systems were presented as specific aids for developing appropriate behavior and motivation.

We now turn to another situation: Attention Deficit Disorder (ADD) whose symptoms mimic noncompliance and lack of self-discipline.

However, these inappropriate behaviors may not be true disciplinary/behavioral issues for the child with Attention Deficit Disorder. The non-compliance of the ADD youngster is currently presumed to be based in a neurological condition--specifically the disruption in brain neurochemistry involving neurotransmitters.

It has been found that 3% to 5% of school age youngsters have Attention Deficit Disorder (CH.A.D.D., 1988) and there are generally eight times as many boys diagnosed with the disorder as are girls. Symptoms are inattention, non-compliance, impulsivity and hyper-activity. The noncompliant behavior of the youngster with Attention Deficit Disorder must be distinguished from the willfully noncompliant behavior of the Conduct Disordered youngster.

Willfully noncompliant children can clearly control be-havior if motivated, whereas the youngster with Atten-tion Deficit Disorder may not be able to consistently comply, especially in stimulating or chaotic environ-ments.

Parents are easily frustrated and exasperated by Atten-tion Deficit Disordered youngsters since many of these children display moods that swing quite abruptly.

Teachers do not know how to handle Attention Deficit Disordered children, especially youngsters who are hyperactive. This condition was previously labeled "learning disability," "minimal brain damage" and hyperactivity syndrome."

Ryan

Ryan had always seemed to be an extremely active youngster. It was difficult for him to stay still even as a baby. His parents noted that he seemed to walk without having crawled first, got into everything and the normal child proofing of their home did not seem to be effective.

Ryan had the ability to scale the washer-dryer, reaching detergents on the shelf above. Twice the paramedics were called due to Ryan's ingestion of cleaning agents.

Even though the medical treatment had been uncomfortable, Ryan did not seem to learn from his experience and the parents finally removed all cleaning materials, locking them in a cabinet.

Locks also had to be installed on all doors so that Ryan did not leave the home without his parents' knowledge. On several occasions they had found the door open and Ryan gone! Conscientious neighbors would either bring him home or Ryan's horrified parents would find him riding his tricycle near a heavily traveled intersection.

They became quite concerned for his safety and contacted their pediatrician. The doctor noted that Ryan was, indeed, very curious and active for his age, but felt that at the age of three and one-half years it was too early to diagnose whether he was hyperactive.

The doctor did agree that greater than ordinary supervision would be necessary until Ryan either "outgrew his excessive activity level" or he was diagnosed as having a hyperactivity disorder and was treated.

When Ryan entered preschool, his behavior continued to be uncontrollable. Behavior management techniques helped, but Ryan still did not appear to learn from his experiences and continued to act in a wild, uncontrollable fashion.

His parents finally placed him in a special public school preschool program for behaviorally disturbed youngsters. His behavior was active, but more controlled in this special setting.

119

Ryan was placed, however, in a regular kindergarten class when he turned five years of age. Within two weeks, his teacher had scheduled a parent conference.

It was noted at the conference that his behavior was impulsive (he would throw pencils, shove children in line) and although he seemed to be quite bright, he rarely completed his seat work.

The teacher was concerned that Ryan would harm himself or other youngsters and would not gain academically from his kindergarten year if he could not sit still.

With this information in mind, the parents had another conference with the pediatrician. After reviewing the school's concerns, the pediatrician examined Ryan and diagnosed him as displaying Attention Deficit Hyperactivity Disorder (ADHD).

The parents were relieved to at least have a diagnosis for their son's problems, but they did not understand exactly what Attention Deficit Hyperactivity Disorder was, or what treatment would follow.

Molly

Molly's parents were also concerned about their five-year-old. She had been a delightful youngster, who was very compliant and desirous to please. Her preschool years had been uneventful, except the teachers noted that she daydreamed quite a bit. However, Molly could be brought back to task when her name was called. She was a pleasant child and had many friends.

120

When she began kindergarten her teacher noted that Molly seemed to be very distractible. Even the noise from the air conditioning unit would draw her off-task.

The sounds made by other children sharpening their pencils would distract her and Molly found it very difficult to regain her place on her worksheet.

Molly was beginning to become frustrated with the academic situation. In the middle of her kindergarten year she began to complain of stomach pains and headaches, and her parents noted that she did not wish to go to school anymore.

A conference was then called with her teacher, who described Molly's behavior as very compliant. Nevertheless, Molly often did not complete her work and she appeared to be lost in the classroom.

Intellectual testing had shown that her ability was above average, but Molly was not gaining academically since she often failed to complete her tasks. The parents, teacher and Molly were frustrated. It was then that the teacher referred Molly and her parents to a clinical psychologist.

Psychological testing, as well as observation of Molly within the classroom, suggested that she was exhibiting Undifferentiated Attention Deficit Disorder (UADD).

The psychologist referred Molly and her parents to her pediatrician for medical treatment and set up several therapy sessions for developing a Behavior Management System for Molly.

The pediatrician would deal with the medical management of the Undifferentiated Attention Deficit Disorder while the psychologist would address behavioral management and the teacher would provide the educational therapy. This multi-modal approach to Molly's problems was initially overwhelming to her parents as they began the task of understanding her difficulties.

Attention Deficit Disorder

The diagnostic criteria for Attention Deficit Disorder established by the American Psychiatric Association (1987) are as follows:

A. Inattention (at least three of the following must be evidenced by the child):

- difficulty staying with a play activity
- easily distracted
- doesn't seem to listen
- often fails to finish things that he or she starts
- difficulty concentrating on school work or other tedious tasks which require sustained attention.

B. Impulsivity (at least three of the following must be evidenced by the youngster):

- attention shifts excessively from one activity to another
- has difficulty organizing work
- frequently calls out in class
- difficulty waiting turn in games or group situations
- in need of greater guidance and supervision
- often acts before thinking

C. Hyperactivity (at least two of the following must be evidenced):

- difficulty staying seated
- moves excessively during sleep
- is always on the go
- runs about excessively
- fidgets excessively

D. The problems began before the age of seven years

E. The problems have lasted at least six months

The American Psychiatric Association describes two types of Attention Deficit Disorder: Attention Deficit Hyperactivity Disorder and Undifferentiated Attention Deficit Disorder.

Attention Deficit Hyperactivity Disorder

Attention Deficit Hyperactivity Disorder involves significant disruptive activity, noncompliance, impulsivity and excessive motor activity. Teachers often refer these youngsters for evaluation in the lower grades as their behavior is so disruptive.

Undifferentiated Attention Deficit Disorder

The primary characteristic of this type of Attention Deficit Disorder is *inattentiveness*; hyperactivity is not present. However, these children still manifest problems with organization and distractibility, but temperament may be seen as quiet and passive.

Who's In Charge?

It is felt that Undifferentiated Attention Deficit Disorder is currently under-diagnosed as these children are often overlooked in the classroom since they are not a disruptive problem.

These children may be at higher risk for academic failure than are their disruptive counterparts. As they generally are not diagnosed as early as are hyperactive youngsters their needs may not be met until later years.

Evaluation of Attention Deficit Disorder Using a Multidisciplinary Approach

A multidisciplinary evaluation is necessary for diagnosing Attention Deficit Disorders. The pediatrician, psychologist and teacher all need to be involved.

Educational testing, psychological testing and medical studies of the individual child are generally quite helpful. Differential diagnosis between a Non-Compliant Behavioral Disorder and an Attention Deficit Disorder is an essential prerequisite to effective treatment.

If a child is not performing in the classroom or at home due to an Attention Deficit Disorder, the child may not be processing parent or teacher directions or commands due to inattentiveness.

This is quite a different situation than the noncompliant youngster who has heard and understands what he is supposed to do, but willfully chooses not to comply.

The purposefully noncompliant youngster is best dealt with through the Behavior Management Systems discussed in earlier sections of this book.

The Attention Deficit Disordered youngster requires a multi-modal approach to treatment. Behavior Management Techniques are excellent guidelines for dealing with youngsters with Attention Deficit Disorder, with or without hyperactivity.

Behavior Management is important since these youngsters, even more than children without attentional problems, need high levels of structure and guidance. They tend to be very disorganized and, therefore, charts and Behavior Management Systems provide a great deal of clarity.

Medical Management

Medical management can be very helpful. Psycho-stimulant medication is commonly used in the treatment of both types of Attention Deficit Disorder. However, the use of medication alone in the treatment of ADD is usually not recommended.

Ritalin is the most commonly used medication in treating Attention Deficit Disorder, and it has been prescribed for many years with favorable results and minimal side effects. Other psychostimulants which are often employed are Cylert and Dexedrine.

Antidepressant medications have also been proven successful in treating Attention Deficit Disorder.

The medications are believed to affect the body's neuro-transmitter chemicals, deficiencies which may be the cause of Attention Deficit Disorder (CH.A.D.D., 1988). As with all medications, parents should have a thorough discussion with the pediatrician as to the side effects and dosage levels prescribed.

Improvements in attention span, hyperactivity and impulse control are noted in approximately three-fourths of children who take psychostimulant medications.

School Management

Teachers need to deal very closely with the pediatrician, psychologist and parents of the Attention Deficit Disordered child. A Daily Report Card System is mandatory in order for the child to realize that his behavior is being monitored every period of the school day. Rewards for a good Daily Report Card have been found to be more successful with these youngsters than have punishments.

Attention Deficit Disordered children can be expected to perform well on a Daily Report Card System if they have succeeded in organizing themselves during the day. Consistent reward will remind them that they will have something pleasant to look forward to when they return home if they complete the Daily Report Card.

Recommendations for the Academic Environment

There are many texts available for parents and teachers regarding teaching students with Attention Deficit Disorder.

Several recommendations found to be effective are:

- placing the child away from distracting stimuli

- avoiding changes in schedules and transitions

- trying to produce a stimulus-reduced study area for the youngster

- surrounding children with good role models and

- placement of the student near the teacher's desk as part of the regular class seating arrangement

It is important to determine whether the noncompliant youngster is evidencing an Attention Deficit Disorder or a behavioral disorder in the classroom.

Often, a school observation can be quite helpful. The psychologist who observes the youngster in the classroom can discern whether the child can pay attention if motivated.

The stubborn, noncompliant youngster happily calls out of turn for attention, whereas the youngster with Attention Deficit Hyperactivity Disorder often looks sheepish and embarrassed due to this same inappropriate behavior.

The Undifferentiated Attention Deficit Disordered youngster cannot keep track of where the class is in a book, whereas the noncompliant youngster can, but willfully chooses not to keep up with the others.

Behavioral Management

Often, the use of the Daily Report Card (see p. 78) with an effective consequence being given at the end of the day can help in discerning the correct diagnosis.

Willfully noncompliant children quickly become more organized if the consequence is important, whereas children with attentional problems generally take a longer time to become organized and need greater teacher and parent guidance.

Will My Child Outgrow His Attention Deficit Disorder?

Studies have shown that youngsters do not "outgrow" attentional disorders as previously thought. Depending upon the severity of the attentional problem the prognosis will differ.

Youngsters with mild attentional problems will learn to compensate and their difficulties may not be evident in their teenage and adult years. However, individuals with severe attentional problems will continue to evidence difficulty with impulsivity and distractibility and will generally be more active than their age-mates.

As people mature, they tend to become less active, impulsive and distractible even in severe cases of Attention Deficit Disorder. However, these difficulties will continue to plague them throughout their life. Continuation of medical, behavioral and educational management is imperative.

The adult may need specific vocational guidelines if the attentional difficulty is persistent and severe. Psycho-stimulant medication can continue to be quite helpful. Environmental selection of employment may also be necessary.

For example, the distractible adult who chooses a career in law enforcement may have great difficulty directing traffic at a busy intersection but may function very well in the less stimulating office situation.

Therefore, practical vocational guidance is especially important for teenagers and adults with severe attentional difficulties. Special academic situations are also available for youngsters and young adults with Attention Deficit Disorder.

Beyond the elementary and high school levels, several colleges have recently developed programs for those with learning disabilities and Attention Deficit Disorders that provide a much more structured environment than regular college programs offer.

In addition, intensive tutoring is available that can be quite helpful to the distractible college student. Parents of children with significant attentional disorders should explore the special educational and vocational avenues available to them.

The Hyperactive Child As An Adult

Some studies have addressed what happens to Attention Deficit Disordered youngsters as they grow to adulthood. Adults who were diagnosed as having Attention

Deficit Disorders as youngsters tended to be more disappointed, pessimistic and lacking in self-confidence than a control group. As a group, their social skills also tended to be somewhat impaired.

Employers did not seem to be as disappointed in these adults with Attention Deficit Disorder as had their prior high school teachers. This may be based in the extreme demands present in the academic situation as compared to the less structured requirements of the vocational setting.

The study published in 1986 entitled Hyperactive Children Grown Up (Weiss and Hechtman) noted that approximately 33% to 50% of youngsters with Attention Deficit Disorder continued to have some of these difficulties in adulthood.

These individuals displayed more substance abuse and anti-social behavior than did a control group. In addition, these adults tended to continue to have shorter attention spans, lower impulse control and more mood swings than did their counterparts.

Attention Deficit Disorders and Learning Disabilities

The child with Attention Deficit Disorder often appears to have a learning disability. About ten percent of children in the public school classrooms are eventually diagnosed as having a learning disability (difficulty in processing information). Children with Attention Deficit Disorder have an even higher incidence of learning difficulties than found in the general child population.

Difficulties in understanding or in using language lead to problems in the youngster's ability to perform in the classroom. Difficulty in performing mathematics and in writing, spelling and reading are often symptomatic of a learning disability.

Attentional problems as well as learning disabilities can lead to difficulties in understanding or in using spoken or written language. This is why youngsters with Attention Deficit Disorder are often confused with those with a true learning disability.

Often, the Attention Deficit Disordered child who begins a regimen of psychostimulant medication no longer will evidence a learning difficulty as his attentional processes become more functional.

Emotionality Of The Child With Attention Deficit Disorder

Attention Deficit Disordered children often appear to be immature and insecure. Academic difficulties as well as social difficulties resulting from impulsivity and distractibility often lead these youngsters to develop poor self-concepts. These children are perceived to be unmotivated in school, although their apparent lack of motivation is often misleading.

If this child continues to have difficulty paying attention and completing his work, he will eventually expect to fail to complete assignments and not persevere when faced with uncomfortable tasks.

Psychosomatic complaints (headaches and stomach-aches) often occur at this stage as the youngster becomes frustrated with his school failure.

The youngster's frustration may require psychological treatment due to self-esteem difficulties. A poor self-concept may result in feelings of failure, depression and disappointment with life.

In addition, the parents of children with Attention Deficit Disorder often need a great deal of support. This support is available not only through pediatricians, school counselors and psychologists, but also may be found in parent support groups throughout the country.

There appears to be a genetic component underlying this disorder. Often children diagnosed as having Attention Deficit Disorder will have a sibling with similar problems and one of the biological parents may also display distractibility, impulsivity or overactivity. It is very difficult for the impulsive parent to deal effectively with the impulsive child and psychotherapy for both individuals is often necessary (Friedman and Doyle, 1987).

Once it is ascertained that the youngster is evidencing an Attention Deficit Disorder (with or without Hyperactivity) the parents need to become involved in a structured treatment plan as soon as possible.

It has been found that youngsters with Attention Deficit Hyperactivity Disorder who also evidence a Conduct Disorder often develop anti-social problems such as substance abuse and illegal activities in adolescence.

Placing a youngster on a Behavior Management Program as early in life as possible will help to avoid a Conduct Disorder in adolescence as well as lowering the possibility of teenage delinquent activity.

The youngster with Attention Deficit Hyperactivity Disorder most likely will not develop severe disciplinary problems in adolescence if a multidisciplinary treatment approach has been followed during his childhood years.

Chapter 7

Is There a Typical Child?

There are two gifts parents can give a child: one is roots and the other is wings.

Author Unknown

Statistically speaking, there is not a typical child and therefore there is not one set of guidelines that will work in every aspect for every youngster. Children vary in terms of personality traits, intelligence levels and physical demeanor. Therefore, the notion of a typical child is not realistic.

Regardless of individual differences, all children need a great deal of structure and organization in their lives. In this book the willfully disobedient child has been discussed along with the naturally compliant youngster.

It was noted that Behavior Management Systems are effective in working with both types of children. A Behavior Management System is even more important when working with psychopathological or delinquent youngsters.

The bottom line is that all children need to know where their limits lie and the extent of their boundaries. Youngsters continually need to be informed of the positive consequences they will obtain for behaving

135

appropriately and the negative consequences they will receive for misbehaving.

Pushing of limits is a basic law of human nature. It cannot be underestimated in terms of importance. People respond due to the consequences of their behavior.

In the short run there may be times when it does not appear that a person is behaving in a certain way due to a certain consequence. However, when one explores the entire picture, human behavior is largely motivated by consequences, both negative and positive.

Therefore, parents are very special people indeed. They need to be alert throughout their children's youth by watching behaviors closely and ensuring that their children receive appropriate consequences.

Chapter 2 discussed inadvertently rewarding inappropriate behaviors. It was noted how easy it is for youngsters to feel rewarded for undesirable behaviors when parents are not conscience of how they administer consequences to youngsters.

"Grandma's Rule" suggested that youngsters not be rewarded until they have completed their expectancies. These are rules of behavior which pertain across decades and centuries. The perceptive parent is one who is realistic, practical and accepting of what human nature has to offer.

It is the parent who feels that they or their child does not need to conform to these rules of human nature who will have a difficult time with child rearing.

Realizing the nature of their child's individual personality and the extent of the boundaries needed for the particular child is extremely important. As noted in previous chapters, some children need a very rigid approach in their upbringing.

If one allows an *if-then* child a gray area, watch out! They will take it and run with it. Rules will be abused and communications will be distorted. Other children can be given many gray areas and much flexibility and they will continue to behave appropriately.

The decisive factors are based in the maturity, moral development and self-discipline of the individual youngster.

In addition, the age of the child is quite important. Young children are not able to organize as effectively as older children. Immature adolescents cannot make as well thought out plans as can mature adolescents.

We find that immature adults often make very poor decisions, especially those individuals who have failed to receive negative consequences in their earlier years for making impulsive decisions.

Once the parent has accepted the basic premise of this book: that youngsters respond to the consequences of their actions, the parent can become less emotional regarding their child's difficulties and begin to solve problems more effectively.

Many parents are overwhelmed with anxiety and guilt, feeling that if they had only done something differently, their children would be less selfish or less egocentric.

These parents are paralyzed by negative emotion. Once they realize that their child's personality is partially biologically based, then the parent can seek out the best environmental consequences for the particular youngster.

For example, a parent who continually laments that her strong-willed five-year-old will not comply and spends most of her time wringing her hands and trying to reason with the youngster is not going to get far.

On the other hand, the parent who has accepted her child as a strong-willed stubborn young man, but who sets clear boundaries and presents clear consequences for him, will be more successful in motivating the youngster toward appropriate behavior.

Too many parents define parenting skills in terms of how well their children behave. There is some truth to this in that parents who set strong limits and firm boundaries tend to have better behaved youngsters. However, many children are, by nature, more stubborn and noncompliant than others.

It is important to ascertain which type of child one has and to then decide how much gray area, if any, the youngster can handle.

It is the parents' job to teach the child. Children will change their behaviors when their parents change their expectations. If a parent expects a child to develop self-control by high school, the child will if the stage is set appropriately.

For example, consider the parent who uses a Daily Report Card System with the youngster, continually checks on the child's organizational ability within school and expects that the child will be organized at home. This child will most likely evolve into a self-controlled young adult.

This book has been written for all parents, the mothers and fathers of stubborn, noncompliant youngsters as well as parents of easy going children. It is hoped that the reader has accepted the premise that children's self-control and self-discipline is largely a learned behavior; one that is taught mainly through the home environment.

The second premise, which is of equal importance, is that children with good self-control will develop into adults who are self-disciplined and productive. It is the exceptional young adult who has led a chaotic adolescence and then "sees the light" as an adult, finishes high school and college and becomes successful.

There are individuals among us who are like that. However, the majority of youngsters evolve into the type of adult whose seeds were planted in their early years.

Youngsters who were taught self-control at an early age develop and understand self-discipline naturally as adults. Most likely these youngsters will also pass this gift on to their own children and will perpetuate the positive approach to disciplining children.

Dr. Scott Peck in his book entitled The Road Less Traveled (1978), notes that "Discipline is the basic set of tools we require to solve life's problems. Without discipline we can solve nothing, and with some discipline we can solve only some problems. With total discipline we can solve all problems." (pp. 15, 16).

When parents are themselves undisciplined and therefore offer undisciplined role models for their children, the tools for the development of self control are not passed on to the next generation; hence the transmission of irresponsible values and impulsivity from parent to child.

This impulsive, irresponsible life style will follow them into and through adulthood. Breaking the cycle of low frustration tolerance, irresponsibility and self-indulgence is a societal mandate for the twentieth century.

Parents cannot look to educators, ministers, politicians or pediatricians to teach their children responsibility and self-discipline. It must come from the home environment. Consistent, strong, well-disciplined parents are the prescription for the evolution of self-disciplined successful youngsters.

Indeed, it is the only way to live. Families in which children are in charge are chaotic, unpleasant environments for <u>all</u>--not just for the parents.

Children are happier, more successful, and more self-confident when they know the rules and when they realize that they can achieve them.

Let us give our children the opportunity to succeed.

Let us love them, guide them, and most importantly let us provide an environment rich with opportunities to explore and to grow within clear boundaries.

References

American Psychiatric Association. *Diagnostic and Statistical Manual of Mental Disorders.* Third Edition, Revised. Washington, DC: American Psychiatric Association, 1987.

Bodenhamer, G. *Back In Control.* New York: Prentice-Hall, 1988.

CH.A.D.D. Education Committee. *Attention Deficit Disorders: A Guide for Teachers.* Plantation, FL: CH.A.D.D., 1988.

Clark, L. *The Time-Out Solution.* Chicago: Contemporary Books, 1989.

Dobson, J. *Dare to Discipline.* New York: Bantam Books, 1982.

Dodson, F. *How to Discipline with Love.* New York: Signet, 1978.

Friedman, R. J. and Doyal, G. T. *Attention Deficit Disorder and Hyperactivity.* Danville, Illinois: Interstate Printers and Publishers, 1987.

Kagan, J. Essay. *Psychology Today,* 1987.

Peck, M. S. *The Road Less Traveled.* New York: Touchstone, 1978.

Silverman, M. and Lustig, D.A. *Parent Survival Training.* N. Hollywood, CA: Wilshire, 1987.

State Education Performance Chart Supplement. United States Department of Education, 1989.

Weiss, G. and Hechtman, L. T. *Hyperactive Children Grown Up*. New York: Guilford Press, 1986.

ORDER FORM

Who's In Charge? A Positive Parenting Approach to Disciplining Children is available in quality bookstores. If you prefer to order by mail, please send request to:

Lindsay Press, Inc.
P. O. Box 6316
Clearwater, FL 34618-6316

Please send _____ copies of *Who's In Charge? A Positive Parenting Approach to Disciplining Children* @ $12.50 each.

Name_____

Address_____

_____

City/State/Zip_____

Phone (   ) area code _____

Please add $2.00 for shipping and handling.
In Florida, please add $.75 for sales tax.
Send check or money order. No cash or COD's please.

For quicker response
with VISA and MasterCard
telephone order to:
1-800-438-1242, ext. 538
or North Carolina residents only:
1-800-532-0476, ext. 538